HISTORIES OF THE UNEXPECTED
World War II

HISTORIES OF THE UNEXPECTED
World War II

Sam Willis & James Daybell

Atlantic Books
London

First published in Great Britain in 2019 by Atlantic Books,
an imprint of Atlantic Books Ltd.

123456789

A CIP catalogue record for this book is available from
the British Library.

Hardback ISBN: 978-1-78649-775-8
E-book ISBN: 978-1-78649-776-5

Printed and bound by CPI Group (UK) Ltd, Croydon, CR0 4YY

Atlantic Books
An Imprint of Atlantic Books Ltd
Ormond House
26–27 Boswell Street
London
WC1N 3JZ

www.atlantic-books.co.uk

For

Kate   *Felix*
&   *&*
Alice   *Bea*

CONTENTS

Everything

HAS A

history

EVEN THE MOST

unexpected

OF SUBJECTS...

... and *everything*

LINKS — TOGETHER

IN

unexpected

WAYS

A PERSONAL NOTE

At *Histories of the Unexpected*, we believe that *everything* has a history – even the most unexpected of subjects – and that everything links together in unexpected ways.

We believe that the itch, crawling, clouds, lightning, zombies and zebras and holes and perfume and rubbish and mustard – each has a fascinating history of its own.

In this book we take this approach into the Second World War. You will find out here how the history of *carrots* is connected to victory; how the history of *handkerchiefs* is all to do with resistance; and how the history of *pockets* is all about emergencies.

To explore and enjoy subjects in this way will change not only how you think about the past, but also the present. It is enormously rewarding and we encourage you all to join in! Find us online at www.historiesoftheunexpected.com and on Twitter @UnexpectedPod – and do please get in touch.

ACKNOWLEDGEMENTS

This series of books is about sharing great research and new approaches to history. Our first acknowledgement, therefore, must go to all of those brilliant historians – professional and amateur – who are writing today and who are changing the way that we think about the past. You are all doing a fabulous job, and one which often goes unremarked and unrewarded. Thank you for your time, effort, energy and insight. We could not have written this book without you.

Since this book is intended for a wide and general audience, we have chosen not to publish with extensive footnotes. We acknowledge our indebtedness to fellow historians in the Selected Further Reading section at the end of the book, which is also intended as a spur to further research for our readers.

We would like to thank the many colleagues and friends who have generously offered ideas, guidance, support and sustenance, intellectual and otherwise: Darren Aoki, Harry Bennett, Anthony Caleshu, Lee Jane Giles, Jim Holland, the Lord John Russell; and among the twitterati, @HunterSJones, @RedLunaPixie, @KittNoir and @Kazza2014.

Collective thanks are also due to Dan Snow, Dan Morelle, Tom Clifford and the fabulous History Hit team for all their support and encouragement; as well as to Will Atkinson, James Nightingale, Kate Straker, Jamie Forrest, Gemma Wain and everyone at Atlantic Books.

We would also like to thank everyone (and there are hundreds of thousands of you) who has listened to the podcast or come to see one of our live events and been so charming and enthusiastic.

Most of all, however, we would like to thank our families, young and old, for everything they have done and continue to do, to cope with – of *all things* – a historian in their lives.

But we have created this book for you.

Sam and James

Isca – Escanceaster – Exeter
The Feast of St Benedict – 8-Dhū al-Qaʻdah 1440 – I.VII.MMXIX – 11 July 2019

WORLD WAR II:
AN INTRODUCTION

J. Howard Miller's 'We Can Do It!' poster from 1943

WHAT WAS WORLD WAR II?

Between 1939 and 1945, some 100 million people became directly involved in a global conflict fought on a massive scale that involved more than thirty countries. The lives of countless millions more were indirectly affected. More than 60 million died, many of them civilians. Six million of those were Jews murdered in the Holocaust. Over 25 million are known to have been killed in the Soviet Union alone, and more than 15 million in China. All of this happened because the Axis powers of Germany, Italy and Japan were opposed by a conglomerate of nations known as the Allies and led by Britain, America, Russia and China; but during the course of the war, over sixty countries – at one stage or another – fought to oppose the Axis powers. At the same time, several states such as Spain, Portugal, Sweden, Switzerland and Turkey preferred to remain neutral.

It was the most devastating conflict the world has ever known, with the major powers harnessing their most deadly ideologies and technologies into a killing machine that included conventional weaponry alongside chemical and biological warfare, strategic bombing, genocide, starvation and massacres, and which culminated in the dropping of the atomic bomb.

The war was fought from the Arctic to the Antarctic, across seas and trade routes. It was fought on all fronts and in multiple arenas: in mainland Europe, throughout Asia, Africa and the Far East, as well as in the Mediterranean, the Middle East, the Pacific and the Atlantic. It was fought with boots and armoured tanks on the ground, carriers and destroyers at sea, bombers and fighters in the air, and with a whole host of ingenious devices utilized in the shadows of a secret war. It was fought in cities, villages, deserts, mountains and jungles, under the sea as well as on it. It was also fought in the mind, through propaganda, ideology and influence.

Outside of the main operational theatres, the war had far-reaching tentacles of influence on the economic and industrial output of each nation involved. The conflict was not experienced simply by the combatants in the field, air and oceans, but was also fought on the 'home front', where immeasurable contributions were made on all sides to the war effort – whether it was air-raid wardens administering first aid to a bleeding, blitzed city, or mothers mending, 'making do' and improvising family meals from meagre rations, or muddy-fingered gardeners fighting the war with a spade – literally digging for victory. This blurring of the boundaries between civilian and military had a profound impact on the way that people lived their everyday lives. It disconnected families and disrupted working conditions, pulling things apart, but at the same time forces working in the opposite direction drove people together in love and comradeship. The Second World War is certainly about death and loss, but it is also about life and gain.

WHEN WAS WORLD WAR II?

The dates of the conflict are traditionally bookended by the German invasion of Poland, which led to the declaration of war by Britain, France, Australia and New Zealand against Germany in September 1939, and the surrender of Japan in September 1945. But a broader perspective that still focuses on military conflict might look to 1937 and the start of the Second Sino-Japanese War, or to 1936 and the outbreak of the Spanish Civil War, or to 1935 with Italy's invasion of Abyssinia, or even as far back as 1931 with the Japanese seizure of Manchuria. And in each and every case, diplomats and politicians fought their own wars before the actual fighting broke out – a time when pens were guns, and words bullets. The clearest example of this was during the period of appeasement before the outbreak of the Second World War, when for four long years between 1935 and 1939 a sequence of British prime ministers, leading an army of diplomats and politicians, fought desperately to contain the rise of fascism in Hitler's Germany and Mussolini's Italy. Throughout this period, Britain was militarizing in readiness, and many other powers were preparing for war.

When the war ended depended entirely on where you were. The war in Europe ended with VE (Victory in Europe) Day on 8 May 1945, which marked the unconditional surrender of Nazi Germany. It was not, however, until the next day that the German forces occupying the Channel Islands capitulated, and the war continued to be fought elsewhere in the world for many months. Japan surrendered on 15 August, bringing the war to an official end. This became known as VJ (Victory over Japan) Day or VP (Victory in the Pacific) Day. But despite these official declarations, some kept fighting – not knowing of their nations' actions – and others continued to do so in spite of the peace. New wars, all born one way or another from the Second World War, broke out in Korea (1945), Vietnam (1945), Indonesia (1945), Iran (1945), the Philippines (1946), Greece (1946), Romania (1947), India (1947), Palestine (1947), Czechoslovakia (1948) and Burma (1948), some of which were not resolved for many years, and some of which have never been resolved – not least the Israeli-Palestine conflict, which began as a direct result of the war and the subsequent establishment by the United Nations of the Jewish state of Israel in Palestine. The Cold War of the 1950s – a long period of international brinksmanship and fighting – was also a direct result of the Second World War.

For those survivors whose wartime experiences were actually contained between 1939 and 1945, many continued to relive the war in their minds through the trauma they experienced. The war lodged like a splinter in their minds, profoundly affecting their beliefs, thoughts and behaviour for the rest of their lives.

Over seventy years on, memories of the severity and sacrifice live on as the war is remembered and commemorated by those born long after it ended.

A WORLD OF EVIDENCE

A war of such magnitude means that the Second World War is one of the best-documented periods in history. The conflict impacted upon almost every aspect of civilization, and an overwhelming body of evidence survives: official documents, informal writings, art, poetry, oral history, living testimony, artefacts, film, audio, architecture and archaeology. The mile upon mile of documentary evidence means we can forensically reconstruct military operations in precise detail; chart the technological development of munitions and machines; understand policy-making at the heart of the Third Reich; study the impact of popular propaganda from newspapers, newsreels and wireless reports; and we can also learn about children's experiences of the war and the impact that the conflict had on countless aspects of society. The challenge for the historian, therefore, is not only to pick a topic but also to pick a way to explore that topic – as each different approach will raise and answer different questions. For this reason, the Second World War is something of a historical kaleidoscope: looked at like *this* you see one thing, like *that* you see another, and that constant process of discovery is what makes the period so absorbing.

The scale of the war's evidence and its relative proximity in time also makes this a deeply personal war for many of us today. Countless families have their own private archives from the period, perhaps stored in a cupboard, perhaps stuffed in a box in the attic, perhaps displayed for all to see in a frame; you may not have formally noticed it, but the war inadvertently made historians and archivists out of millions of us. Survivors have their own memories, and the generations are still close enough for those who did not experience the war to be able to remember very clearly those who did – and their stories.

We were both born in the 1970s and remember grandparents who lived through the conflict, which makes the period particularly relevant and close for us – regardless of the fact that we are professional historians. James's father was born midway through the war, and he has a collection of postcards from his own father, who was fighting on the continent; they were written in pencil and partially in code to avoid being censored. Sam has diaries, uniforms, medals, flags, weapons and photographs from his grandparents, all of whom experienced the war in unique ways; as well as his own collection of memories of talking to them about their experiences. Private collections such as these shed light on the experiences of so many, and can be found in the homes of countless families across the world.

A WORLD OF INSIGHTS

The scale of the conflict and the extent of the surviving evidence also mean that the Second World War can be understood from a diverse range of viewpoints: historians have written about it from the perspective of nationality, race, religion, gender and sexual orientation. There is work on the experiences of children and the elderly and the disabled, and a whole range of occupations or other groups: those who fought, the pacifists who didn't fight, and those who remained neutral; prisoners incarcerated for their nationality, faith, ethnicity or sexuality; medics and the wounded; volunteers, slaves, labourers and professionals; politicians and diplomats; entertainers, artists, authors, poets and composers; the cowardly and the courageous; the traumatized and anxious; the elated and the shamed.

Through such varied work, historians have been able to recreate the 'lived experience' of the war to see how the conflict played out in so many different minds. How did a Japanese soldier fighting on the front line in the jungles of Burma experience the war? Or a Japanese civilian living in the US or Canada, forced to spend the war in an internment camp? Or the pilot of a B-52 bomber dropping incendiary bombs on packed cities? Or a German mother of no fewer than twenty children, striving to raise a family 'worthy' of the German Reich? Or a Japanese father reading a letter from his only son, penned minutes before a mission in which he deliberately flew his plane into an enemy ship? Or an evacuee child taken from her parents and put on a train to the country during the worst of the Blitz? Each of these perspectives is unique in its own way, but cumulatively they build a complex picture of the war; a mosaic of glittering details.

AN UNEXPECTED APPROACH

Traditionally, the Second World War has been presented in a very straightforward way, concentrating on military campaigns, warfare and military technology, and following the well-known personalities, events and themes. We think, however, that the period comes alive if you take an *unexpected* approach to its history.

Yes, battles, bombs and bravery all have a fascinating history, but so too do handkerchiefs, furniture, Mozart, insects, blood, cars, mothers, King Arthur, gates, suicide, Zen Buddhism, cancer, puppets, pockets, cows, deafness, darkness, rubble and even carrots!

Each of these subjects is fascinating in its own right, and each also sheds new light on the traditional subjects and themes that we think we know so well.

Are you ready for an infusion of historical knowledge? Then let's start with the history of blood...

·1·

BLOOD

Jüdisches Selbstbekenntnis

Der Judenmetzger führt das Rind zum Schächten

Anti-Semitic article attacking Jewish kosher slaughter in
Der Stürmer, Number 14, 1937

Blood is all about recruitment...

— PARLIAMENTARY RECRUITMENT IN BRITAIN —

In rousing political speeches made prior to and during the course of the war, spilled blood was synonymous with the sacrifice that British troops made for the nation. In 1938, Neville Chamberlain famously returned from Munich, disembarked from his plane to massed crowds, waved a piece of paper and proclaimed that he had achieved 'peace with honour. I believe it is peace for our time.' The paper was the Anglo-German Declaration, signed by Chamberlain and Hitler, confirming the details of an agreement between Germany, Italy, France and Britain known as the Munich Pact, which permitted Nazi annexation of the Sudetenland in western Czechoslovakia. It was the culmination of Chamberlain's policy of appeasement.

The subsequent debate in parliament on 5 October between pro- and anti-appeasement MPs several times dwelled on the image of bloodshed. Colonel Sandeman Allen praised the prime minister, saying 'there is no blood on our hands, and there might easily have been so', mentioning a speech the previous night that had quoted the first chapter of Isaiah: 'When you come to make prayers, do not have blood on your hands.' This argument was countered equally effectively by the Welsh MP David Grenfell, who invoked the honour of sacrificing one's life for the good of the country. He claimed that negotiation with Hitler would lead to the 'threat of extermination' for many in Eastern Europe, especially in Czechoslovakia. 'I can sympathise', he intoned:

> with those gallant people who are willing, in the face of overwhelming odds, to stand as men have stood before and shed their blood that the people may be free when they themselves are dead and gone. The willingness to make

that sacrifice has been denied to them. They are asked not to indulge in this proud act of self-immolation, but to refrain from exercising this privilege of men for the sake of the peace of Europe, and they are rewarded with a threat of extermination with the certainty almost of the complete dissolution of their collective life.

He championed here the valour and bravery of men – among them the Welshmen he represented – who were willing to lay down their lives so that others could be free.

Once the war had started, this motif of spilled blood in the service of protecting one's country found its most powerful rhetorical performance in Winston Churchill's speech to parliament on 13 May 1940. Churchill borrowed his imagery from earlier speeches from two very different sources: the Italian revolutionary Giuseppe Garibaldi (1807–82), and the former president of the United States, Theodore Roosevelt (1858–1919).

Appeasement

A diplomatic policy during the period 1935 to 1939 of making political and material concessions to Nazi Germany and Fascist Italy in order to avoid armed conflict. This led to the signing of the Munich Pact on 30 September 1938. Appeasement was opposed by the Labour party and political left, and by Conservative dissenters like Winston Churchill, who argued: 'You were given the choice between war and dishonour. You chose dishonour and you will have war.' He was right. The following year, Hitler annexed the rest of Czechoslovakia in March, and in September invaded Poland, leading to the outbreak of the war.

The speech was made three days after Churchill became prime minister and came to be famous for the phrase 'I have nothing to offer but blood, toil, tears and sweat', which he had also used in a speech delivered to his cabinet when he met them earlier that day. The purpose of the parliamentary speech was to recruit support for a new all-party government. In it, he outlined the government's policy:

> I would say to the House as I said to those who have joined this government: 'I have nothing to offer but blood, toil, tears and sweat'. We have before us an ordeal of the most grievous kind. We have before us many, many long months of struggle and of suffering.
>
> You ask, what is our policy? I can say: It is to wage war, by sea, land and air, with all our might and with all the strength that God can give us; to wage war against a monstrous tyranny, never surpassed in the dark, lamentable catalogue of human crime.

His rousing words were met with some support on the backbenches, and William Spens, Conservative MP for South Kensington, was so inspired that he referred to them directly in his own response:

> I assure my right hon. Friend the Prime Minister and all his colleagues that, whatever we on the back benches on this side of the House can do, by supporting them, to help in winning the war, we intend to do. Blood or tears or toil or labour, we shall give most gladly.

BLOODTHIRSTINESS

Taken one way, the spilling of blood – especially if it was one's own – was an act of great courage and valour, an image used to strengthen national resolve. But bloodshed could also be presented as something much darker and more menacing, and could be used to demonize the perpetrators. Nowhere is this more clearly witnessed than in the Nazi propaganda that sought to recruit to its banner by whipping up a hysterical and rabid hatred of the Jewish people, who were often presented as bloodthirsty and were even portrayed to children as 'bed bugs' or 'bloodsuckers'.

Their relationship to meat – as slaughterers, butchers and eaters – was one of the key ways in which the Nazis sought to represent Jews as impure and a danger to 'civilized' German society. While on the one hand vegetarian associations were banned in Nazi Germany, key members of the party including Hitler himself paraded their vegetarianism, and Nazi animal protection laws safeguarded animals from ill-treatment. In this scenario, ideologically the Nazis became the protectors of animals, while Jews were vilified for harming them. This negative stereotyping of Jews focused on the act of slaughter, and especially the ways in which they spilled animal blood.

The Nazis were obsessed with kosher slaughter, in which the animal is killed by slitting its throat and allowing the blood to drain out, so the meat can be eaten without blood – as is required by Judaism. To the Nazis this caused needless added suffering to animals, and in their eyes it allowed them to characterize the Jews as vicious animal-haters. Images connected to kosher slaughter featured in the vehemently anti-Semitic newspaper *Der Stürmer*. An article in 1937 pictured a Jewish man dressed in a long black cloak guiding a cow towards a building, carrying the caption 'The Jewish butcher leads the cow to the slaughterhouse'. The men in the background, presumably gentile Germans, look on with distaste and alarm.

In a later issue, the subject was further twisted by Nazi propagandists in a more forthright and vivid way. In 1938, a photograph of a dead cow hanging upside down was featured with the title 'A Horrible Image'. The accompanying article described in gruesome detail the dispatching of the animal – which was slit across the throat to the vertebra, causing blood to spurt all over the walls – and the animal's attempt at escape, concluding 'what a horrible death'. The religious nature of slaughter was then introduced, with three photographs of a rabbi opening the wounds and pulling out a lung, into which he must blow to see if the beast is healthy. If it is, then the meat is deemed kosher; if diseased, it would then be sold to non-Jews to eat.

Thus, in an inaccurate caricature of their relationship to blood, Jewish people were branded by Nazis as inhumane killers, and their religious practices were mocked and turned against them as a symbol of their 'impurity': a powerful tool indeed for recruitment to the Nazis' anti-Semitic mission.

Der Stürmer

Translated as *The Stormer*, this weekly German tabloid newspaper was founded in 1923 by Julius Streicher, a prominent member of the Nazi party. Although not an official Nazi publication – unlike the *Völkischer Beobachter* – the periodical was strongly anti-Semitic, and published a diatribe of propaganda that cast Jews, Catholics, Communists and monarchists in a bad light.

– BLOOD DONORS AND THE AMERICAN RED CROSS –

Alongside the rhetoric and propaganda of bloodshed as a vehicle for recruitment, there is a more practical side to its history, to do with blood donation. One of the most remarkable achievements in this area during the war was the work of the American Red Cross Blood Donor Service. From the point of the US entry into the conflict in 1941, the Red Cross collected blood from millions of ordinary donors across the country. This was then processed in laboratories to turn it into plasma and serum albumin substitutes (a liquid component of blood, and the key protein critical in the treatment of many types of trauma), which were then shipped along with blood supplies (including whole blood donations) around the world.

The whole operation was an enormous logistical feat, jointly run by the military and the Red Cross. By the end of the war, some 6.7 million volunteers had donated more than 13 million pints of blood. To run this operation, the Blood Donor Service itself had to recruit more than 100,000 volunteer staff, as well as myriad doctors and nurses.

According to one of the first historians of the organization, deliveries involved a range of methods to transport the blood to the furthest theatres of fighting: it was delivered 'on the backs of mountain-climbing mules, on litters carried by natives in the jungles of the South Pacific, and in planes which at times dropped the plasma by parachutes to troops on land isolated from normal supply'. So successful was the campaign that General Dwight D. Eisenhower commented: 'If I could reach all America, there is one thing I would like to do – thank them for blood plasma and whole blood. It has been a tremendous thing.'

·2·
KING ARTHUR

Susan Ashley (Evelyn Dall) and Arthur King (Arthur Askey) examine 'Excalibur' in a scene from the 1942 film *King Arthur Was a Gentleman*

King Arthur is all about the
Battle of Britain...

You might think King Arthur, the legendary British king whose feats are recounted in medieval romances, would be an unlikely hero of the Second World War. But in 1940, as the British fought for their survival in the Battle of Britain, Arthur – along with his fabled Knights of the Round Table, his wizardy sidekick Merlin and his lover Guinevere – started to appear prominently and repeatedly in the consciousness of the British public. They were figures raised from the mists of history to inspire and lighten the hearts of the people in these darkest of days.

A TIME OF CRISIS

This resurgence of interest in Arthurian tales occurred at a time when the threat of Nazi aggression cast its shadow across the English Channel. In June 1940, the British Expeditionary Force was evacuated from Dunkirk, France fell to the Germans and the invasion of Britain was planned.

This was the month in which Churchill delivered his famous speech declaring Britain's intention to resist German aggression, rousing Britons to fight on the beaches, landing grounds, fields, streets and hills, and never to surrender. When it came, the battle was fought in the skies of southern Britain, as the Germans sought to force Churchill's hand into a negotiated peace. The bombing of British airfields soon gave way to the bombing of British cities.

It was in this fevered atmosphere that Arthur reappeared. He was a king whose traits and story could be used in a number of ways to bolster the nation's spirit. As a legendary figure, this ancient king was a man of exceptional morality and indomitable spirit who appealed widely to a broad cross section of the population, bridging social and cultural divisions within British society. He fought invaders; he created prosperity; he was a man with a special affinity with the nation – closer even than martial leaders with more tangible historical bona fides such as the naval hero Horatio Nelson or the Tudor queen Elizabeth I, both of whom had shepherded the country in times of crisis. Most importantly of all, however, Arthur's story involved a messianic return – a promise that he would rise when called upon, at a time when Britain needed him most.

British Expeditionary Force (BEF)

The name for the British army sent into Europe at the beginning of the Second World War to support the French against German invasion. The Allied forces failed to repel the invaders, and in May–June 1940 the Germans conquered France, Belgium, Luxembourg and the Netherlands. In the process of the German advance, the BEF was pushed back towards the sea where a total of 224,320 British troops were evacuated from Dunkirk between 26 May and 4 June 1940.

CHURCHILL'S FAVOURITE

At the height of the country's fight for survival, the time was ripe for Arthur's return to the fray, and in the summer of 1940 he began to appear across the media, in political speeches, letters in the press, saga-length poems, radio plays, children's magazines and even in the cinema.

One of his keenest champions was the prime minister Winston Churchill, who before the outbreak of war had been writing an ambitious multi-volume history of Britain and its colonies around the world entitled *A History of the English-Speaking Peoples*. The early chapters were written in 1937–9 and would have been reasonably fresh in Churchill's mind, not least the rousing passage in the fourth chapter, 'The Lost Island', which dealt with the period immediately after Roman rule:

> And wherever men are fighting against barbarism, tyranny and massacre, for freedom, law and honour, let them remember that the fame of their deeds, even though they themselves be exterminated, may perhaps be celebrated as long as the world rolls round. Let us then declare that King Arthur and his noble knights... sustained by valour, physical strength, and good horses and armour, slaughtered innumerable hosts of foul barbarians and set decent folk an example for all time.

For Churchill, the war in Europe was the very moment he had been imagining. In a speech to parliament on 4 June 1940, he equated Britain's servicemen to Arthur's knights, mentioning the Knights of the Round Table by paraphrasing Alfred, Lord Tennyson's *Idylls of the King* (1859–85), a series of twelve narrative poems which retold the legend of King Arthur: 'Every morn brought forth a noble chance, and every chance brought forth a noble Knight.'

In Churchill's mind, the threat that Britain now faced was just such a 'noble chance', and he cast it in a chivalric light. Ranks of young British 'knights' would not just emulate the glorious deeds of Arthur's medieval heroes – but surpass them.

MEDIEVAL COMBAT

The chivalrous exploits of Arthurian legend that inspired Churchill's speeches were seized upon by other political commentators, who also reached out to Britain's noble past – and saw in the battles played out in the skies above southern England something of the honour and pageantry of medieval tournaments. The parallels were evident. These were minor engagements, short starbursts of violence, but on their outcomes rode much larger fates.

Moreover, in both jousting and aerial dogfights, life and death was put on public display: the few fought while the many watched. In 1940, many of the battles took place in daylight and low enough to be clearly seen. People watched, necks craned back, as the warriors charged at each other in the sky. The *Guardian* newspaper on 16 September 1940 reported how, in London: 'Thousands in the centre of the capital cheered wildly as they watched the Spitfires send a big German bomber hurtling to destruction.'

German planes were shot out of the sky at Victoria, Kennington and Streatham. In one combat at the time, a Spitfire destroyed a German bomber and promptly performed a victory roll, upon which 'the crowds below cheered madly and danced with joy as the bomber fell'.

This bewitching parallel between the medieval and the modern was captured most magnificently by the cartoonist Sidney Strube. On 27 August 1940, two days after German bombers had first dropped bombs on the centre of London, and British bombers bombed Berlin in retaliation, Strube published a cartoon in the *Daily Express* which showed a medieval knight in the clouds, carrying the colours of the RAF and smiting a Nazi dragon with a sword of freedom.

THE KING OF DRAMA

The BBC also got in on the act. Just the previous year they had broadcast a six-part dramatization of the English author T. H. White's novel *The Sword in the Stone* (1938) – a fantasy of King Arthur's boyhood – including specially commissioned music by the leading English composer of the age, Benjamin Britten (1913–76). In 1940, they made an even more significant commitment to broadcasting the Arthurian theme, commissioning from the playwright Clemence Dane seven separate dramas, gathered together under the title *The Saviours*.

The series was a broad historical survey of British heroism and inspirational military leadership. It began with a drama dedicated to King Arthur's sage and adviser, Merlin, who became the narrator for the entire *Saviours* series, thus creating a strong thread of Arthurian legend throughout each of the dramas – regardless of the historical period in which they were set. The second part, *The Hope of Britain*, was dedicated entirely to Arthur himself. A significant foundation stone of the series was that Dane (incorrectly) identified modern Britons as being descendants of 'native' 'Ancient Britons', who she presented as being ethnically distinct from Anglo-Saxons with German heritage. Through this historical sleight of hand, Dane could present Arthur's battles with the Anglo-Saxons in terms of protecting England from hordes of 'German' invaders, a point that was readily understood at the time.

Arthur even made it onto film. In 1942, Gainsborough Pictures made *King Arthur Was a Gentleman*, featuring the immensely popular comedian Arthur Askey (1900–82). The film was a thinly disguised patriotic message emphasizing the need for everyone to be involved in the war effort. Its main character is the loveable – but short, nervous and short-sighted – Arthur King. At first, Arthur is unable to sign up (yes, because he is too short, too nervous and too short-sighted) but then he finds his way to the front. While training in Cornwall, Arthur finds a sword – which he names Excalibur, the name of Arthur's legendary sword in the medieval romances.

Arthur takes his sword with him everywhere – even to the front line in North Africa. There his heroism knows no bounds, and, wielding Excalibur, Arthur single-handedly captures some Germans in the act of poisoning the British army's water supply. Here, therefore, is a slightly different take on the Arthurian legend – this is not Arthur as King of the Britons, but Arthur as *everyman*; a direct cry for help aimed at the civilian population, though the message is disguised in pure 1940s slapstick and farce, including plenty of cross-dressing and bad puns.

Clemence Dane (1888–1965)

The pen name of Winifred Ashton, a prolific British novelist and playwright and a pioneering feminist. As well as radio plays for the BBC, she wrote scripts for Hollywood. In 1946 she won the Academy Award for Best Original Motion Picture Story for the film *Perfect Strangers*, a wartime romance in which the main characters - played by Robert Donat and Deborah Kerr - are transformed by the war for the better.

THE REAL EXCALIBUR

One crucial part of Arthur King's story, however, does ring true – and that is his fondness for, and use of, his sword. Just like Arthur King, the serving British army officer John Churchill (1906–96) took this principle onto the battlefield itself, claiming that 'Any officer who goes into action without his sword is improperly dressed.' Nicknamed 'Fighting Jack Churchill' and 'Mad Jack', Churchill saw himself as a medieval knight reborn. And not only did he fight with his sword, but he also used a traditional longbow. An expert archer, having represented Great Britain at the 1939 World Archery Championships, he used his medieval weaponry at the battle of L'Epinette in the retreat from northern France in 1940. With his company trapped, Churchill led his men to safety through the German lines, in the process of which he shot a German staff sergeant through the chest with a barbed arrow fired from his bow. He was subsequently awarded the Military Cross.

The poet and playwright Lord Dunsany (1879–1957), who wrote numerous significant poems at this time, joined in with this Arthurian spirit – if not with the actual weaponry. In 'The Song of an L.D.V.', which so charmingly brings all of these Arthurian themes together, Dunsany describes how, as a sixty-three-year-old preparing to join up with Local Defence Volunteers – the forerunner to the Home Guard – he sought out and dusted off his old sporting gun, and named it afresh as Excalibur:

> Dull instruments we use to slay,
> Compared with those of old.
> And not a weapon of to-day
> Is lovely to behold.
>
> But since it was King Arthur's aim
> To keep his Britain free,
> And feelings pretty much the same
> Inspire the L.D.V.

Although of armour we have none,
Nor shield nor sword nor spur,
I've given my old sporting gun
The name Excalibur.

CANCER

Nicht er sie ....
sie frißt ihn!
Überschrift:
Der Kettenraucher

Nazi anti-smoking propaganda poster, Reine Luft, 1941

Cancer is all about German fascism...

In the 1920s and 1930s, German doctors – who were among the finest in the world in the field of epidemiology – realized that cancer was on the rise. This posed a problem that troubled the Nazis. It was a disease that struck at the heart of an idealized, well-functioning fascist state by threatening its workforce, posing a drain on its resources, polluting the purity of the German body and defying a cure.

A NAZI OBSESSION

One of the foundation stones of Nazism was the belief that – in this new, wealthy and industrialized nation – everyone had a duty to work, and that the state was responsible for allowing this work to take place. An important part of that responsibility concerned the welfare of the workers, who were a resource that benefited the state. If workers were unable to work to their full potential because they were incapacitated by cancer, then cancer should be targeted.

Cancer was viewed as an important topic for Nazi doctors to study not only because it reduced the nation's output, but also because it put the nation – which operated a system of national health insurance – to great and 'unnecessary' expense in treating those who suffered from the disease. Smoking-induced lung cancer was a particular concern, because it was not just something that affected individual smokers; it impacted on the collective group via passive smoking. It was the kind of antisocial activity that went directly against the Nazi belief of 'all for one and one for all' in the 'people's community' of Germany they named *Volksgemeinschaft*.

Volksgemeinschaft

The notion of a 'people's community' became popular in Germany during the First World War, but was radically overhauled and set centre stage by the Nazis – who used it to suggest a mythical unity or soul that united all Germans and linked them to their land. It became a byword for German unity and racial purity in the face of internal and external threats, such as Marxism, Jews and the Allies.

Another major tenet of National Socialism was racial purity, and cancer – with its unpleasant, invasive and uncontrollable tumours – was clearly a threat to the long-term Nazi vision of physical perfection. It was a threat that needed to be addressed.

The seemingly incurable (or at least uncontrollable) nature of cancer was the type of challenge that the Nazis embraced with gusto. The late 1930s was a time of immense energy and dynamism in Germany. Their eyes set firmly on the future, the Nazis were intent on building a happier, healthier Germany, and nothing would stand in their way. Nazi propagandists spoke constantly in terms of 'radical', 'permanent' or 'final' solutions – phrases we know for their distressing associations with the Holocaust, but which were also applied to health. Professor Dr Immanuel Gonser, the head of the Anti-Alcoholism Association, summed it up in 1933:

We Germans stand at an important turning point: new men are shaping the destiny of our fatherland, new laws are being created, new measures put into place, new forces awakened. The struggle touches on everything that has been and is unclean.

The new state was uniquely set up to wage this war: tackling cancer was a political problem as much as it was medical, because to tackle it would require a huge increase in medical surveillance and intrusion into the private lives of Germany's citizens. It would require mass record-keeping, mass screening and mass diagnosis.

A wealth of material survives illustrating how this was sold to the public. One inventive poster shows a man tinkering under the bonnet of a car. The accompanying text explains: 'Every automobile gets a regular check-up; that is obvious. Shouldn't the much more complicated machine of the human body also get regular check-ups?' Another example demonstrates how the Nazis blended their policies together, and how when it came to smoking this included their racial policies. Part of a campaign to ban smoking from waiting rooms, the poster shows a door marked *Diensträume* ('waiting room') with the foot of a military-style boot kicking out a cigarette, cigar and pipe. The cigar includes a caricature portrait of an African on the label – an attempt to characterize smoking as a vice of 'degenerate' people of colour.

EXCEPTIONAL MEDICINE

Added to all of this was a well-developed culture of high-quality medical and scientific research that already existed in Germany. If there was any country in the world to take on cancer in the late 1930s, it was Germany – after all, this was the country from which half the world's Nobel Prizes had originated, as well as many of the world's most significant patents. This was the country that had nurtured scientists responsible for the development of the television, the electron microscope and computers, among many other landmark technological inventions that define the twentieth century. It was a land of research, innovation and ingenuity, and that infrastructure and extant talent pool allowed the Nazis to embrace the challenge of waging a war on cancer with a level of determination far greater than any other nation had embraced it before.

Pre-war Germany and the Nobel Prize

In the 1930s alone, German-born scientists were awarded four Nobel Prizes for chemistry and four for physiology or medicine. They included Gerhard Domagk (1895-1964), who discovered the first commercially available antibiotic, and Otto Loewi (1873-1961), who made significant advances in our understanding of neurotransmitters.

Funding was sought and provided at every level of research. More than 1,000 doctoral theses were produced in the twelve years of Nazi rule, and that level of investment in cutting-edge medical research paid real dividends. Nazi Germany became the world leader – decades ahead of any other nation – in the understanding of the causes and prevention of cancer. Their researchers were not only the first to discover the link between lung cancer and smoking, but also the links between cancer and sunlight, X-rays, uranium and food dyes. They found evidence, for example, linking bladder cancer with dye-working; skin, bone and blood cancers with X-rays; lung cancer with uranium mining; and arsenic cancers with the work of vintners, glass-workers and steelworkers.

Politicians, meanwhile, set about tackling cancer's impact via a mass programme of prevention that included several high-profile campaigns: one to encourage people to stop smoking; another to promote regular health check-ups; another to urge people to eat cleaner or more natural foods with less sugars, fats and preservatives, and to drink purer water; and one advocating regular exercise.

It certainly helped that Hitler believed passionately in an active and healthy lifestyle – he was a vegetarian teetotaller who loathed smoking, something that was made famous by Nazi party literature. One party magazine from 1937, *Auf der Wacht*, carried a formal portrait of Hitler looking extremely serious and diligent, and the caption below read: 'Our Führer Adolf Hitler drinks no alcohol and does not smoke... His performance at work is incredible.'

Hitler's mother, Klara, with whom he had been exceptionally close, had died of breast cancer when he was still a teenager. The family doctor, the Jewish Eduard Bloch, later recalled his treatment of her:

> One day Frau Hitler came to visit me during my morning office hours. She complained of a pain in her chest. She spoke in a quiet, hushed voice; almost a whisper. The pain she said, had been great; enough to keep her awake nights on end. She had been busy with her household so had neglected to seek medical aid. Besides, she thought the pain would pass away... An examination showed that Frau Hitler had an extensive tumour of the breast... I shall never forget Klara Hitler during those days. She was forty-eight at the time; tall, slender and rather handsome, yet wasted by disease.

She died on 21 December 1907 when Adolf was just eighteen. Throughout his time in power, Hitler remained personally interested in the fight against cancer. In 1941, the Institute for the Struggle Against Tobacco Hazards was established at the University of Jena, supported by a 100,000 Reichsmark grant from the Reich Chancellery.

THE SURPRISING BENEFITS OF MUSTARD GAS

The rearing threat of fascism also helped to encourage break-throughs in the treatment of cancer in America, and inspired the discovery of cancer chemotherapy. The resurgence of a militant Germany in the 1930s raised fears in America that chemical warfare, such a potent weapon in the First World War, might be used in any new conflict. This directly led American scientists to undertake new research into the effects of one of the most common chemical weapons of the previous war: mustard gas, which had been responsible for 1,205,655 non-fatal casualties in the First World War and 91,198 deaths.

In the process of that research it was discovered that, when the patient was exposed to mustard gas, profound lymphoid and myeloid suppression occurred, and it was subsequently proved by two researchers working at the Yale School of Medicine that mustard gas suppressed the division of certain types of cells. That discovery was then applied to cancer cells, which are distinctive because of their uncontrollable and rapid division.

The first clinical trials of mustard gas as a treatment for cancer took place in 1942 at Yale, on a patient suffering from non-Hodgkin's lymphoma. He came from Connecticut and worked in a ball-bearing factory, but was known in the sources only as 'JD'. JD's tumour masses were significantly reduced by the gas, though the treatment was not sufficiently advanced to save his life. Nonetheless, the chemical warfare agent in mustard gas – nitrogen mustard – was subsequently recognized as the world's first effective treatment for cancer, and it is still used for the treatment of certain types of cancer today.

·4·
CARROTS

'DOCTOR CARROT the Children's best friend' poster

Carrots are all about victory…

SEEING IN THE DARK

It is a well-known fact – and a scientifically proven one – that carrots are good for the eyesight, but as part of the Allied campaign for victory in the air, the British perpetuated the myth that carrots actually helped you to see in the dark.

The job of British pilots during the Blitz was made all the more tricky because of the wide-scale blackout that was imposed, which plunged their world into darkness. Flying at night was disorientating for pilots, and in a Commons debate in January 1940 the MP Sir William Brass, himself a former RAF pilot, warned that 'you cannot bomb accurately at night'.

One RAF pilot, John Cunningham (1917–2002), who flew for the specialized night-fighter unit 604 Squadron, was celebrated for his achievements. He became widely known as 'Cat's Eyes' due to his success in shooting down enemy planes – he ended his career with a tally of twenty planes downed, three 'probable' and six damaged. Cunningham's spectacular success was put down to eating an excess of carrots – or at least, that was the line that the ministry fed to the newspapers.

604 Squadron

Established in March 1930 as a day-bomber unit, the No. 604 Squadron RAF became well known during the Second World War for radar-controlled night-fighter operations. It was disbanded in 1945, as part of a reduction of the British Armed Forces towards the end of the war.

Such propaganda was part of a deliberate ploy to hide from the Germans the real reason for the British strike rate – they were equipped with new radar that could intercept enemy aircraft. Nonetheless, the notion that carrots were good for night vision was perpetuated broadly throughout Britain in a series of campaigns, such as an advert which appeared in *The Times* on 6 February 1942 and ran with the slogan 'Carrots keep you healthy and help you see in the blackout'. Another reason for this kind of advertising was to raise morale during a time of fear and darkness, and also to encourage the consumption of carrots – which were healthy, readily available because they were not rationed, and easy to grow. They may not have given pilots night vision, but they represented an indirect route to victory.

DIGGING FOR VICTORY

The German blockade of food-supply ships during the war led to acute shortages of various commodities. This privation led to a system of rationing, in which the population was strictly limited in the quantities of foodstuffs they were allowed to buy. Citizens had to register with particular food shops and were given a ration book containing coupons. The shopkeepers were provided with enough stock for their registered customers, who handed over their coupons when they did their shopping in exchange for their allotted amount for that week. Rationed foods included sugar, tea, meat, cheese, preserves, butter, margarine, lard and sweets. Carrots and other vegetables were not rationed throughout the entire course of the war.

Alongside rationing, a campaign to fight the war on the 'kitchen front' was introduced; victory would be achieved through the home gardener and the kitchen cook. Lord Woolton, the Minister of Food, declared in 1941: 'This is a food war. Every extra row of vegetables in allotments save shipping. The battle on the kitchen front cannot be won without help from the kitchen garden.' The British took to the challenge – which became known as the 'Dig for Victory' campaign – like rabbits in a cabbage patch. What ensued was nothing less than a nationwide horticultural mobilization, with men, women and children recruited into the garden.

Homeowners were encouraged to be self-sustaining by planting vegetables in their gardens, and the number of allotments rose from 930,000 in autumn 1939 to 1.7 million by 1943. Wasteland, sports fields and golf courses were requisitioned and planted, and even Buckingham Palace and Windsor Castle had their own vegetable patches, instigated by King George VI. So successful was the programme that, by 1943, domestic vegetable production was a whopping 6 million tonnes a year.

The Dig for Victory campaign was intended not just to boost morale on the home front during the trials of the war, but also to impose a degree of state control over the production of food domestically. Thus, poster campaigns that encouraged healthy eating and providing food for the sake of hungry children were circulated alongside government advice that instructed people what to grow in winter and summer, when to sow and when to crop. The idea was to ensure orderly cropping and a year-round supply of vegetables. The 'Dig for Victory Leaflet No. 1', for example, advised the planting of five rows of carrots a foot apart from each other, as a maincrop in rotation with other vegetable crops over a three-year cycle.

During this period, the carrot became a symbol of the Dig for Victory campaign, with the character Dr Carrot used to persuade people to eat more of this nutritional vegetable. A 1941 poster campaign depicted a bespectacled, friendly-looking carrot carrying a briefcase labelled 'VIT A' with the title 'DOCTOR CARROT, the Children's best friend'. The Disney cartoonist Hank Porter even designed a whole carrot family for the food ministry to use in their campaign. So successful were they in encouraging people to grow the crop, it is estimated that in 1942 alone there was a surplus of 100,000 tonnes of carrots.

KITCHEN THRIFT

The campaign for victory on the home front extended from the gardens into the kitchen, and great culinary minds turned the orangey root vegetable into 'delicious' and nutritious dishes for the family. Wartime cookbooks are full of handy tips for how to eke out one's rations and make mouth-watering meals from what was to hand. In fact, the Ministry of Food's 'War Cookery Leaflet No. 4' was devoted in its *entirety* to recipes using carrots, which it considered 'one of the most valuable of all our root vegetables and to-day we are apt to take them a little too much for granted and to forget how rich they are in protective elements'.

Ministry of Food

Set up in 1939 just after the outbreak of war, the Ministry of Food was overseen for much of the war by Lord Woolton, a prominent businessman who was appointed Minister of Food in April 1940. The foremost task of the ministry was to coordinate the rationing of food during the conflict, and the minister was in charge of 50,000 employees and a network of a thousand local offices which controlled all food sold in Britain.

The leaflet's recipes include some involving raw carrots, which could be used in all manner of ways: grated and placed in a sandwich, or as an ingredient in an economical winter salad. Carrot caps (the green knobbly bit we all cut off today) could likewise be thriftily saved and turned into a delicious salad, and carrots could be steamed, boiled and braised. There were instructions for carrot soups, carrot savoury, carrot croquettes and what was known as 'War-and-Peace pudding', which was an alternative to Christmas pudding – just made with carrots instead of mincemeat. Finally, there were instructions on how to carefully store carrots, because victory would not be achieved on the home front if food was wasted or left to rot. The secret was to lift them from the ground in good condition, place them in a dry shed, and lay alternate rows of carrots and sand in a pyramid shape. 'It is', readers were informed, 'a wise plan to rebuild your pyramid at least once during the winter.'

Carrots were also promoted as natural sweeteners at a time when sugar was hard to come by and rationed at just eight ounces per week. Desserts like carrot puddings, flans and cakes were recommended for those with a sweet-tooth, and a drink called 'carrolade' (a bizarre combination of carrot and swede) could also be found on wartime menus, though frankly it sounds wholly unappetizing. For children there were carrots on a stick – a substitute for ice cream, which was almost unheard of during the war.

·5·
MOZART

German stamp commemorating 150 years since the death of
Wolfgang Amadeus Mozart (1756–91), first issued 1941

Mozart is all about propaganda...

AN AUSTRIAN OR A GERMAN?

The Nazis saw Mozart as a gift from history. From the late 1930s onwards, and peaking in 1941 on the 150th anniversary of the Austrian composer's death, Mozart became nothing less than a cultural weapon that was wielded with some sophistication by Hitler and his Minister of Propaganda, Josef Goebbels.

Mozart's value lay in the fact that he wasn't actually German at all, but Austrian – and the identity of Austria lay at the heart of Nazi foreign policy. In 1938, Hitler launched a policy called *Heim ins Reich* (meaning 'back home to the Reich'). It encouraged all Germans living outside of Nazi Germany, in particular in Austria, Poland and Czechoslovakia, to bring those areas – once under German control, but lost in the aftermath of the First World War with the signing of the Treaty of Versailles – back into Greater Germany. Hitler also had a personal interest in Austria, because he was born in 1889 in Braunau am Inn, a small town in what was then Austria-Hungary. In 1938, Hitler finally achieved his long-cherished dream of reunifying Austria with Germany; on 12 March, Austria was annexed in a process that became known as the *Anschluss*.

The *Anschluss* gave the Nazis the opportunity to rebrand famous Austrians as 'Germans', and there was no one more famous than Mozart, who could now be repackaged as a true German national icon.

The *Anschluss*

The *Anschluss* was the political union of Austria and Germany in 1938. On 12 March, German troops occupied Austria, and a month later the union was confirmed by a public referendum held in Austria. The question posed was 'Do you agree with the reunification of Austria with the German Reich that was enacted on 13 March 1938 and do you vote for the party of our leader, Adolf Hitler?' The official result was 99.73 per cent in favour with a 99.71 per cent turnout. Voters were put under immense pressure from the formidable Nazi propaganda machine, but historians believe there was also a strong desire among the majority of Austrians to welcome Hitler and unite.

A FESTIVAL HEADLINER

It was particularly advantageous for the Germans that Mozart was born in Salzburg, the location of one of the most important musical festivals in Europe, which had been held each summer since 1920 (and still is). The Nazis seized this opportunity with a carefully constructed and massive publicity drive to bring the once-Austrian-but-now-German Mozart to the ears of everyone they could.

Salzburg hosted Mozart-themed concerts and events for the entire year, with a particular highlight being the festival in August, at which Goebbels personally laid a wreath in the room where Mozart had been born. The propaganda minister had also insisted that somewhere between 10,000 and 20,000 German soldiers should be given priority attendance, an opportunity to bring Mozart to the ears of the troops.

Most of the significant cities in Germany followed suit and had their own Mozart-themed celebrations on various scales. Most impressively, Frankfurt put on eleven of Mozart's operas, presented in their order of composition from *Idomeneo* (*Idomeneus*, 1781) to *Die Zauberflöte* (*The Magic Flute*, 1791). Leipzig went further still, putting on almost *all* of Mozart's twenty-two operas over four months. To link these geographically dislocated celebrations together and to inspire people to attend, that year the Nazis also produced two lengthy radio series chronicling Mozart's life, with performances by the leading orchestras marshalled by leading conductors, cleverly conceived to be transmitted from the very buildings in which the pieces had first been performed.

For those not lucky enough to actually be there, some of the concerts were broadcast on the radio and were even picked up by troops on the front lines. This was considered of inestimable value, particularly so in the darkest times of the war. An article in the popular Nazi newspaper *Völkischer Beobachter* published on 31 January 1943 – an immensely difficult time for the Germans, with the British restarting their aerial bombardment of Berlin and the Russians finally beginning to lift the German siege of Leningrad – explained how Mozart's music conveyed 'an artistic experience which lifts it out of the horrors of daily life into light and blessed heights', a perception that was also shared by Goebbels. For him, Mozart was a man who could do nothing less than 'raise the spirits of a tormented humanity and remove it to a better world'.

One officer serving on the Eastern Front wrote in a letter of how one such concert inspired him and his men who were 'living in the rocky Tundra amidst the Asian hordes and beneath the bullet-raked tanks, burst armoured wagons, stinking corpses of the horses and smashed human bodies'. With their backs to the wall as they held a defensive position and readied for renewing their attack:

[one] misty summer evening found us gathered around a fire, and one of the Comrades was twisting the knobs on the radio receiver so as to bring the voice of our homeland into our circle of men... it was then that we were moved by the ceremonial sounds of the trombone in *Die Zauberflöte* and by the bitter sadness of Pamina which filled an unforgettable summer's night. The Salzburg master reminded us soldiers anew what we were defending . . . Salzburg truly radiates light into the hard hearts of warriors and newly ignites the spirit of war in them.

ADMIRING THE ENEMY'S MUSIC

For all of the Nazi regime's desire to associate themselves with Mozart, the British had no qualms at all in playing Mozart – or, in fact, any German music. This was radically different from the First World War, when there had been vociferous objections to hearing the 'enemy's music'.

During the war, lunchtime recitals were held five days a week at the National Gallery in Trafalgar Square, organized by the British pianist Myra Hess. In all, 1,968 recitals were put on during the six and a half years they were held, and were attended by 824,152 people. In October 1940, at the height of the Blitz, when London was suffering a month of nightly bombing by the Germans, works were performed by the greatest Austro-German composers: four Beethoven concerts, three Bach and three more by Mozart. In a letter to the government written by the gallery in May 1941, asking for funds to make the location safer, it was noted how 'Miss Hess makes a great point of the propaganda value of the concerts.'

German music was even played by the British within earshot of the Germans themselves. Writing to the *Musical Times* in February 1944 from the German prisoner-of-war camp Stalag Luft VI, Sergeant Gordon Barnes described a music society that had been formed there. They played recorded music and also live music, having cobbled together an orchestra of thirty. As well as pieces by British composers such as Vaughan Williams and Benjamin Britten, they played Beethoven, Bach and Mozart, 'a present repertory of tolerable standard'.

Stalags

'Stalag' was an abbreviated form of the German word *Stammlager*, which was itself an abbreviation of the lengthy German word for a prisoner-of-war camp: *Kriegsgefangenen-Mannschafts-Stammlager*. Stalags were notably different from other German internment camps, as they contained only enemy combat personnel from non-commissioned ranks. They were then subdivided according to land, sea or air. 'Luft' camps were for captured airmen, the *Luft* being short for the German word for its air force: *Luftwaffe*.

The main concern for the British was not who wrote the music, but that music of any type should continue to be performed – a celebration of culture and civilization in the darkest of times. This opinion was not shared by all, however. In July 1940, the Canadian Broadcasting Corporation refused to broadcast any German or Italian music, a move that aroused considerable ire in the British press. In November of that same year, Ralph Hill, music editor of the *Radio Times*, published a piece in which he described the idea of banning enemy music as 'childish, totalitarian, and anti-musical', and evidence of 'ignorant and misguided patriotism'. He stated firmly that 'the value of a piece of music has nothing whatsoever to do with the character of [its] country'.

Hill was by no means alone in his opinions, and the playing of German music became something of an anti-Nazi rallying cry in Britain: the clear implication being that, by celebrating the achievement of historic Austro-German composers, you could make the historical point that not *all* Germans were evil – that Nazism was the problem.

DARKNESS

·6·
DARKNESS

'BLACKOUT means BLACK' poster reminding citizens of complete
blackouts as a civil defence procedure, c.1942

Darkness is all about crime...

THE BLITZ

From 7 September 1940, the German air force began an unprecedented programme of aerial attacks on British cities. As the nation's capital city, London was the primary target for German bombers, but other large industrial centres such as Bristol, Liverpool, Birmingham, Glasgow and Coventry were also attacked. War had been brought to the home front during the First World War in the form of aerial bombardment – forcing civilians to confront the reality of living under threat – but never on a scale such as this. At the start of what became known as 'the Blitz', London underwent a sustained and concerted attack and was bombed on fifty-seven *consecutive* nights – an attempt to pulverize the country into submission.

One of the defensive measures adopted – both in Britain and in Germany, where German citizens cowered under the threat of British aerial bombardment – was to adopt a 'blackout'. In theory, every light in every home, office block, school, factory, shipyard, ship and vehicle was to be either extinguished at night or hidden by heavy blackout curtains and shutters that were fixed to windows and doors in order to prevent the light from 'escaping'; this was a period in which light itself was incarcerated. The intention was to make it more difficult for enemy pilots to find their targets.

The blackout in the UK, unprecedented in geographical scale and duration, lasted for 2,062 nights, from 1 September 1939 – two days before war was declared – until 23 April 1945, and it profoundly affected how life was lived and experienced. The journalist Mea Allan (1909–82) wrote:

I stood on the footway of Hungerford bridge across the Thames watching the lights of London go out. The whole great town was lit up like a fairyland, in a dazzle that reached into the sky, and then one by one, as a switch was pulled, each area went dark, the dazzle becoming a patchwork of lights being snuffed out here and there until a last one remained, and it too went out. What was left us was more than just wartime blackout, it was a fearful portent of what war was to be. We had not thought that we would have to fight in darkness, or that light would be our enemy.

NEW TYPES OF CRIME

The war brought with it a whole host of new crimes. The blackout was one of the reasons for this growth, because of the legal measures enforced by the Air Raid Precaution (ARP) wardens, who were organized by each and every local council and were responsible for policing the public putting-out of lights. In his memoirs, Roy Sudlow, who experienced the war as a ten-year-old in Manchester, said that he would remember the cry 'Put that light out!' to his dying day, so regularly did he hear it.

By the end of the war, almost one in fifty Britons (no fewer than 925,000 people) had been convicted of a 'lighting offence', a type of crime which peaked in 1940 during the Battle of Britain, when there were 300,000 successful prosecutions. All home-owners had to hide light behind thick black curtains or paint their windows with black paint; shopkeepers had to black out their windows and provide a means for customers to enter and leave their premises without any light escaping. Lights on train carriages and in railway stations were also blacked out. To begin with, no lights of any description were allowed on the street after dark, though small torches were later permitted – but only if the beam was masked with tissue paper and pointed downwards. Red glows from lit cigarettes were banned. This was all harshly enforced: on one occasion, just after war had broken out, a man who struck a match to look for his false teeth at Bridgend Station was fined ten shillings.

Cyclists had to hood the lights on their bicycles, and at first no headlights were allowed for cars driving at night, but this soon proved extremely dangerous for pedestrians and drivers alike. In 1939, the king's surgeon, Wilfred Trotter, wrote in the *British Medical Journal* that by 'frightening the nation into blackout regulations, the Luftwaffe was able to kill 600 British citizens a month without ever taking to the air, at a cost to itself of exactly nothing'. The number of deaths peaked in 1940 at 9,169 – which equated to one dead for every 200 cars on the road. Thereafter, dipped headlights that shone through covers containing horizontal slits were permitted.

The wardens' job of policing light was easier in rural communities than cities. A reporter for Mass Observation observing the Oxfordshire village of Burford noted that there was a difference between town and country life:

The effect of the local warden coming and ticking one off for not blacking out in a village is rather one of feeling that a village delegate is coming to censure you and that you, the outsider, have behaved rather shamefully. In London, on the other hand, the feeling rather tends to be that when a warden knocks on your door he is a damn nuisance and you suppose you've got to see to it about the curtains.

One of the worst offenders was in fact the government itself, as one of the peculiarities of the blackout legislation was that offences in government-occupied buildings were immune from prosecution. In November 1939, Mass Observation conducted a survey of the government offices in Whitehall to see how many failed to comply with the blackout regulations, with the number of 'imperfectly blacked out windows' counted:

Admiralty 17
Arch 17
Home Office 35
War Office 4
Buildings in Storey's Gate (Office of Works etc) 29
Charles St. 45

And also the number of windows 'poorly blinded':

Admiralty Arch 5
Foreign Office 6

It is unlikely that these particular transgressions were deliberate attempts to undermine the state's control and light the way for German planes, but others were – ranging from the deliberate illumination of windows to setting fire to haystacks.

Mass Observation

Founded in 1937, Mass Observation was a research project on contemporary life unlike any that had gone before. A national panel of volunteers wrote diaries and replied to regular questionnaires and other similar tasks, and a team of paid investigators recorded behaviour and conversation in a wide variety of locations and circumstances. It continued until the mid-1960s, but its value was appreciated anew in 1981 when the project was revived. It is still running today, and the Mass Observation Archive is one of the most important historical archives in Britain.

Another type of crime that became prevalent with the blackout and bombing was looting. Bomb sites were ransacked for valuables, or personal items that had been strewn by the winds of war were simply picked up and pocketed. In practice, however, most of the crimes of this nature concerned the theft of small items of little value. Two types of looters were particularly noticeable. The first group identified as active under cover of darkness were the youth – most of them first-time offenders. Juvenile crime soared in the blackout; in London, a full 45 per cent of looters were under the age of twenty-one, and this age group also seem to have been particularly responsible for the wilful damage of public shelters. There was also, however, a noticeable problem with people in the positions of trust newly created by the unique war situation, who took advantage of their roles. Air-raid wardens, ARP demolition or rescue workers, auxiliary firemen and even policemen were among those convicted for looting, and received harsh penalties.

The darkness also created opportunities for more traditional crimes to flourish. Prostitution rose in perfect conditions for it to do so: a world swathed in darkness, populated with mass gatherings of people. And while it was intended to keep people safe from enemy aircraft, the blackout had the unusual effect of making them feel less safe around each other. The darkness created fear in many forms, but most powerfully in the fear of personal attacks such as rape, mugging and murder.

Historians still debate the actual crime figures. Did crimes actually increase, or did the reporting of them increase? Were people now made more aware of the dangers of the streets because of their darkness? Did new ways to break the law increase the crime rate disproportionately? What *is* certain is that the crime rate exploded during the war. Between 1939 and 1945, reported crimes in England and Wales rose from 303,711 to 478,394, an increase of 58 per cent. We also know from countless diaries and newspaper accounts that the fear created by the darkness, exacerbated by the anxiety of the bombing threat, was real; it changed the atmosphere of night-time Britain. In particular, reports of assaults against women became more common, as well as following and stalking. In September 1939, a female reporter for Mass Observation wrote:

> Just before my stopping place the bus stopped at a pub and several people got on including a youngish looking man who dithered about and eventually sat immediately behind me and tried to attract my attention. When I got off the bus he followed and walked on my heels (a terrifying experience in the black-out). When I could stand it no longer, I turned and flashed my torch full in his face and then ran for home. Felt very shaken. Had bath and turned in.

HATE CRIMES

One important way in which darkness was experienced by hundreds of thousands of civilians was time spent in mass public shelters. As the threat continued, thousands took to such shelters, many of which were underground – the worst in pitch blackness, the best dimly lit. In London the Tube stations were used; in Ramsgate, Kent, a whole network of tunnels was built; other shelters were improvised in cellars, basements, railway arches, crypts and underground warehouses.

Ramsgate tunnels

Ramsgate became the home to the most extensive public underground air-raid shelter in the country. A pre-existing Victorian railway tunnel was extended into the chalk cliffs, with a network of seven-feet-wide and six-feet-high tunnels, up to ninety feet deep and totalling almost three miles. As many as 26,000 people could be accommodated in them in times of danger.

On the one hand, such close proximity could create a community spirit; a sense of Britons together against invaders, backs to the wall, making the best of a bad situation. In some of the largest shelters, communities worked together to improve conditions and organize activities – sewing circles, discussion groups, concerts – to keep morale up. At the same time, however, such overcrowding created opportunities for thieves – and in particular pickpockets – and it also served to expose the extant and well-established fault lines in society: divisions of class, race and gender.

In particular, the conditions created the opportunity for the sharp lines of racism – very much part of London life – to become more visible. Nina Hibbin, born into a Jewish family in Essex, worked for Mass Observation. Part of her job was to document reactions to the war among East Enders, and she noted that: 'Race feeling was very marked – not so much between Cockney and Jews, as between White and Black. In fact, the presence of considerable coloured elements was responsible for drawing Cockney and Jew together, against the Indian.' But anti-Semitism also found a ready home in the shelters. Jews were accused of securing the best places in the public shelters – and thus, by implication, of being the first to 'panic and flee' at the first warning of an attack; as well as of controlling the black market and inflating prices. One Catholic weekly newspaper described a large public shelter in Tilbury, Essex, as a 'brothel' where 'the ubiquitous Jew and his family' spread disease.

·7·
CARS

———

Adolf Hitler inspecting the first Volkswagen Beetle off the
production line in Stuttgart, 1936

Cars are all about the war effort...

THE VOLKSWAGEN

The development of the Volkswagen was Hitler's grand vision to provide a robust, reliable and cheap form of motorized transportation that would put German civilians on the roads while at the same time mobilizing the military – key to any future war effort. Inspired by America's Henry Ford and his popular and iconic Model T, Hitler announced his plans for 'people's motorization' at the Berlin Motor Show in February 1933, soon after becoming German chancellor. He promised tax benefits for car owners, and a massive state-sponsored road-building scheme. The following summer, the Reich Association of the German Automobile Industry tasked the automotive engineer Ferdinand Porsche with the job of designing and building the 'people's car' – or *Volkswagen* – under the slogan 'Strength Through Joy'.

Ferdinand Porsche (1875–1951)

Born in Liberec in Bohemia, then part of Austria-Hungary, Ferdinand Porsche was an automotive engineer and the founder of the Porsche car company. He created the first gasoline-electric hybrid vehicle, the Lohner-Porsche, as well as the Volkswagen Beetle and Mercedes-Benz SS. During the Second World War he was instrumental in contributing to the Nazi effort, helping to develop tanks, the V-1 flying bomb, and adapting the Volkswagen Beetle for military use.

At the heart of Nazi plans for mass motorization was the dream of creating a fascist consumer culture, or 'traffic community', that would unite all Germans and erode class differences (with the exception of Jews). Prototypes were produced by 1935, and a Volkswagen factory was built in Wolfsburg in May 1938. The Volkswagen was funded, not through credit as was the case in the US, but by people paying instalments up front. Some 250,000 Germans paid for their cars in advance in this manner – but never in fact received them. The war intervened and the much-promoted people's car became part of the mass mobilization of the German military. In the shadow of war, consumerism was thus replaced by imperialism and militarism.

After war broke out, production at the new factory began on the *Kübelwagen*, which was essentially a Beetle adapted for military purposes. It was manufactured using forced labour, including several hundred workers from concentration camps. Porsche also developed a Type 62 prototype (later known as the Type 82, which was the version that went into full-scale production in 1940), a lightweight military vehicle with no doors but with bucket seats to prevent the driver and passengers from falling out. The *Kübelwagen* was used both by the German Wehrmacht (armed forces) and the Waffen-SS, and was intended for all-terrain driving. The vehicle outperformed other military transport, proving its worth in on- and off-road conditions, as well as in snow and ice. It benefited from having a flat, smooth underbody and good ground clearance, which meant that, with independent suspension on all four wheels, it could cover all manner of surfaces with relative ease. The people's motorcar was thus repurposed to contribute to the Nazi war effort.

AN AMERICAN LOVE AFFAIR

Soon after America's entry into the war, the manufacture of US civilian vehicles stopped, as factories – including the biggest names in car manufacturing, Chrysler and General Motors – switched production to military vehicles. In 1941, more than 3 million cars had rolled off the production lines of US car manufacturers, but from February 1942 until the end of the war almost no vehicles were produced for domestic use. The lack of new cars, combined with the rationing of gasoline for fuel and rubber for tyres (supply of which had been badly affected by the Japanese occupation of the Pacific and its plentiful rubber resources), radically changed wartime America's relationship with the automobile.

Propaganda posters encouraged citizens to drive less often, reduce their speed and to consider car-sharing, all of which were packaged up in the rhetoric of patriotism. For example, one poster showed a torpedoed oil tanker off the Atlantic coast, with the slogan 'Should brave men die so you can drive...?'; while another, from 1941, urged drivers to join a car-sharing club, exclaiming 'When you ride alone, you ride with Hitler!' Women were targeted in a different way, with one newspaper article arguing that cycling and walking was a 'DELIGHTFUL NEW WAY TO REDUCE HIPS', adding 'You'll soon be a finer figure of a woman if you'll just help make gas rationing work!'

'Another tanker torpedoed off the Atlantic coast. Should brave men die so you can drive...?' US poster about gasoline and rubber rationing, 1942

Far from turning Americans away from their beloved cars, the symbol of consumerist individualism, the experience of the Second World War only furthered the attachment by building a sense of demand and putting the automobile right at the heart of what it was to be a patriotic American. Corporate advertising in particular connected sacrifice and non-consumption with patriotism; denying yourself became part of your duty as an American. The Office of Wartime Information (OWI) put out press releases, radio shorts and poster campaigns promoting the car as an essential part of the war effort. Maintaining your car in good working order – despite the shortages – was presented as important, which had a positive impact on the automobile servicing industries. A memorandum from the OWI on carpooling emphasized that 'All car operators have in their possession a valuable unit in their nation's transportation plan... an automobile.' Carpooling was not the unscheduled picking-up of hitchhikers from the side of the road, but a well-organized activity involving friends and work colleagues.

This is not to say that everyone contributed to the war effort in this way, however, and in the motor industry cities of Detroit and Indianapolis there was considerable opposition to laws restricting civilian driving habits. The opinions of those resisting the government plans can be found in letters to officials. Steve Reznik complained to the Office of Price Administration in Washington:

If gas rationing takes effect in Detroit God help those who will have to depend on the Detroit Street Railway System. It's the worst transportation system in the world. Ask those who ride it. They ride it not because they want to but because they have to. They don't own an automobile.

Throughout the war, the car was still presented as the preferred mode of transportation of the American people, and the enforced austerity of the early 1940s meant that there was pent-up demand once the war was over and the domestic car market could once again boom.

ASSASSINATION

Cars were a focus of the war effort in another unexpected way: they were intricately involved in numerous kidnap and assassination attempts that directly affected the war. On 26 April 1944, an operation was launched by the British Special Operations Executive (SOE) and the Cretan resistance with the aim of abducting Heinrich Kreipe, the German soldier in charge of occupied Crete and the commander of Fortress Crete, the strategically important garrison and fortification on the island.

Special Operations Executive

The SOE was a top-secret British organization set up in July 1940 under the Minister of Economic Warfare, Hugh Dalton, amalgamating three secret organizations. It mission was fourfold: to conduct espionage, sabotage and reconnaissance against Axis powers, and assist resistance movements locally. They used indirect means to target the Axis war effort, as well as direct action to cut off supply chains and assassinate military figures.

An abduction team led by the British agents Patrick Leigh Fermor and William Stanley Moss ambushed Kreipe's car en route from his residence, tying up the German and knocking his driver unconscious. They then impersonated Kreipe and the driver – the car acting as a passport – passing through some twenty-two checkpoints before reaching the deserted village of

Heliana, then continued on foot until they were picked up by British motorboats that took them safely to Egypt.

A car was also involved in the assassination of the top Nazi official Reinhard Heydrich, nicknamed by Hitler 'The Man with the Iron Heart', who masterminded the Final Solution to exterminate the Jews. On 27 May 1942 Heydrich was on his way to Berlin to meet Hitler when he was ambushed in his car, a Mercedes-Benz 320 Convertible B, by two Czech soldiers who had been trained by the SOE. His assassins had got wind of his route, which took him through the Prague suburb of Libeň on a road that included a hairpin bend. As Heydrich's car slowed to turn, one of the soldiers opened fire, only for his machine gun to jam. Rather than speeding away from the scene, Heydrich ordered his driver to stop in order to confront his attackers, at which point the other Czech soldier hurled a grenade that exploded at the rear of the car, fatally injuring Heydrich, who later died of his wounds in hospital.

·8·
POCKETS

Woman wearing a Land Army uniform during the Second World War

Pockets are all about emergencies…

THE CARGO POCKET

The 1930s saw a revolution in army uniforms, which were redesigned to make them more functional during combat, and key to this development was the inclusion of pockets that were useful in emergencies. Pockets had been an important part of military uniforms for centuries – stitched into jackets, shirts and coats – but it was not until the early twentieth century that pockets were added to trousers for the first time; this new design was the cargo pocket.

In 1938, the British army adopted a new type of uniform – widely known as 'battledress' or later as No. 5 Uniform – that was practical and functional. It was worn by British forces, as well as Free European forces such as the Free Belgian forces, throughout the war.

Free Belgian forces

Distinct from the resistance movements in Belgium, the Free Belgian forces were a group of soldiers from Belgium and its colonies who, after the surrender of their country to Nazi Germany in May 1940, continued to fight the war alongside Allied forces.

The trousers in this uniform featured a large map pocket by the left knee, and a right upper hip pocket, designed to carry a field dressing. A new-pattern battledress was introduced in 1942, which in early designs included two inside pockets in the shirt, reduced to a single inside pocket in later variations. Troops in parachute and glider units were issued special parachutist trousers, which incorporated two rear pockets for field dressings, as well as a commodious map pocket, lined with chamois leather for its absorbency and softness, and a small knife pocket.

It was not just the British who recognized the versatility of these pockets, and the cargo pocket was also adopted by the US Airborne divisions. In 1942 the commander of the 82nd Airborne Division, Major William P. Yarborough, oversaw the development of a special new uniform aimed to equip paratroopers for the situations in which they would find themselves during the conflict. Alongside newly designed jump boots, new combat fatigues incorporated several extra-large pockets – two on the trousers and four on the jacket.

The pockets were specially designed with the unique equipment and role of the paratrooper in mind. Paratroopers had to carry with them everything they would need in combat, with the average man shouldering over 100 pounds of equipment. They had to carry so much kit that there are reports of US troops on their way to the airfields throwing cartons of cigarettes and loose change from their pockets to the watching crowds in order to lighten their pockets. The list of kit included three K-rations of daily combat food (as well as an extra in the jump trousers), a raincoat, two D-rations or emergency chocolate bars (with three more in the jacket), a TL-122B flashlight with batteries, a bandolier of .30-06 ammunition (as well as two on the chest), a shaving and toiletry kit, a sewing kit, a carton of cigarettes and two 60mm mortar rounds.

Having to carry this amount of stuff meant that pockets were essential for holding those extra items that would not fit into bags or onto belts. The breast pockets of the new uniform, which slanted down and inwards, facilitated easy access for the paratrooper in his harness, while the thigh pockets were large enough to hold essential military supplies. A concealed dual-zippered knife pocket was also stitched into the jacket collar; it contained a three-inch switchblade, which could be used by the paratrooper to cut himself free should he become entangled in the branches of a tree as he landed.

It is estimated that troopers carried almost nine pounds of gear in their pockets, necessitating many to wear pairs of braces in order to prevent their trousers from falling down. In fact, on D-Day, as men jumped out of aircraft under anti-aircraft fire and into a strong slipstream, their pockets were so overstuffed that in some instances the force of the parachute opening split the pockets' seams, scattering their possessions across Normandy. For future jumps, men patched their pockets to reinforce the seams and prevent the same thing from happening again.

WOMEN'S POCKETS

With the emergence of women working to support the war effort, pockets also became a marked feature of female attire, as women undertook what had traditionally been men's work. In some instances, a wife might quite literally wear her husband's trousers (suitably altered) for manual work, since this was considered practical and it meant they could spare their clothing ration tickets for other items. This was a radical change. Until the eighteenth century, pockets were portable fabric bags unconnected to garments, which could be carried or worn under a dress. By the late 1800s, however, designs for dresses reveal patterns for stitching fabric pockets into clothing for women who wished to be seen as independent, and from the early 1900s – as women began to wear trousers – the sight of pockets was not uncommon, though still far from widespread.

With the Second World War, pockets were also part of the official female uniforms that women wore in the many roles that they performed during these years, either as part of the armed services through the women's auxiliary forces or through nursing and other uniformed voluntary organizations. The uniform issued to the Women's Land Army consisted of a hat, overcoat, pullover, two shirts, an overall and a pair of Wellington boots; and those who served in the corps, known as 'Land Girls', were certainly aware of the usefulness of their pockets. Margaret White from London described the practicalities of having pockets in her uniform and remembered the gorgeous summer of 1943, and how she and the farmer she worked for one day went to hoe the cabbage field with bottles of cold tea and cheese sandwiches in their pockets. They could, however, be a source of angst, for pockets came with rules: another Land Girl, Phyllis Rutherford, got into trouble because she was caught with her hand in her pocket while using machinery.

Women's Land Army

First established in 1915 during the First World War, the Women's Land Army (WLA) was restarted in June 1939. This civilian organization placed women in agricultural jobs vacated by men who had left for war. At first, the work was voluntary, but later women were conscripted to work on the land, meaning that by 1944 there were more than 80,000 members.

Some were deeply troubled by women wearing what was seen as male clothing. Until relatively recently, pockets had been seen by many as inappropriate for women's clothing. They were looked upon as unfeminine, and a patriarchal society worried about what women might *conceal* in their pockets. Now, there were further concerns about what this change in clothing actually represented. The new opportunities and roles that the war offered to women created anxieties about them performing men's jobs. The wearing of trousers with pockets, rather than skirts or dresses, challenged traditional patriarchal images of women as domestic helpmeets – and certain sections of society saw this as a threat. In the US, the cartoonist Russ Westover (1886–1966) hoped that women wearing trousers as part of the war effort would not mean that they abandoned the skirt altogether. Other conservative commentators feared what might happen to the home life of the nation. In 1942, Congressman Hoffman of Michigan stated at a hearing of the House of Representatives his fear of women in uniform: 'Take women into the armed services in any appreciable number, who then will manage the home fires; who will do the cooking, the washing, the mending, the humble, homey tasks to which every woman has devoted herself?'

As part of the war effort, governments sought to control the overuse of material in the manufacture of civilian clothing, and this, too, affected pockets. Rules produced as part of the Utility clothing scheme for civilians in Britain stipulated that women's dresses should have no more than two pockets, while in the US the government rules were much stricter. As part of the War Production Board's restrictions and quotas on clothing, they promulgated a 'no fabric over fabric' rule in order to reduce the amount of material used in manufacture. In reality this meant 'no pleats, patch pockets or full skirts, with limited use of embroidery' – in other words, pockets were seen as superfluous for civilian female domestic attire. Restrictions were similarly applied to the size of men's pockets and turn-ups on trousers.

SIREN SUITS AND KANGAROO COATS

During rationing in England, material was at a premium, and there was a culture of 'make do and mend', with wartime clothes needing to be very versatile, and cleverly designed pockets for emergencies incorporated into particular garments. Among these practical items of clothing was the 'siren suit', an all-in-one jumpsuit with a zippered front that could be quickly pulled over one's normal attire in the middle of the night when the sirens sounded and people had to rush down to the public air-raid shelters. Siren suits were a wartime necessity, worn by everyone – even Winston Churchill and Princesses Elizabeth and Margaret.

Over the top of these could also be worn something called a kangaroo coat, which was similar to a cloak and was so named because of the very large pockets – like a kangaroo's pouch – that were used to carry all manner of valuable personal items, which would be stuffed into them upon leaving the house. These large coats were made of thick fabric to keep the occupant warm on cold nights in the air-raid shelter, and they and the siren suits were easily run up at home. Eileen Whitmore from Rushden in Northamptonshire remembered her mother running up siren suits for her and her sister during the war:

> My mother made for my sister and I 'Siren Suits'… so named so that when a siren sounded, my mother could quickly put us in this suit so whatever we were wearing, she could zip us up and off we went… Then carry us down and put us in the Morrison Shelter.

·9·

FURNITURE

Reconstruction of the bookcase at the Anne Frank House in Amsterdam

Furniture is all about protection...

HIDING FROM NAZIS

Behind an ordinary-looking bookcase on the second floor of Prinsengracht 263, Amsterdam, lay the entrance to the secret annex (*Achterhuis*) in which the famous German-born Jewish child diarist Anne Frank lived with her parents, her sister Margot and four other Jewish people, between 1942 and 1944. During this period the Netherlands was under German occupation, and Jews were rounded up and sent to concentration camps. In order to avoid this fate, the Franks hid in a series of rooms in a back extension of this building, which was the premises of the Opekta pectin and spice company. Furniture in the form of a bookcase was what protected them from being found out, and their experiences were shared by countless other Jewish people during the period of Nazi persecution.

German occupation of the Netherlands

Despite its neutrality during the Second World War, and the German guarantee of this neutrality in late 1939, the Netherlands was invaded by German forces on 10 May 1940. Even after brave fighting on the part of the Dutch, they were outmanned and outgunned, with the bombing of Rotterdam forcing them to surrender within days. The country was ruled by a German civilian governor and forced to conform to Nazi rule, including the persecution of the Jews.

In an entry in her diary dated 9 July 1942, Anne describes the conditions in which she and her family lived:

The door to the right of the landing leads to the 'Secret Annex' at the back of the house. No one would ever suspect there were so many rooms behind that plain grey door. There's just one small step in front of the door, and then you're inside. Straight ahead of you is a steep flight of stairs. To the left is a narrow hallway opening onto a room that serves as the Frank family's living room and bedroom. Next door is a smaller room, the bedroom and study of the two young ladies of the family. To the right of the stairs is a windowless washroom with a sink. The door in the corner leads to the toilet and another one to Margot's and my room... So there you are. Now I've introduced you to the whole of our lovely Annex!

At this stage in the diary, the bookcase had not been built, and all that concealed the entrance was a door. It was not until 21 August 1942 that she records the building of the bookcase – overseen by Victor Kugler, one of the Opekta employees who sheltered the Franks. 'Now', she wrote, 'our Secret Annex has truly become secret... Mr Kugler thought it would be better to have a bookcase built in front of the entrance to our hiding place. It swings out on its hinges and opens like a door.'

The house where they hid is now a museum, meticulously recreated from the details of Anne's diary – including the secret entrance. The pine bookcase stands in the corner of the landing, about seven feet tall with three shelves stacked with innocuous-looking lever-arch files from the period, mottled grey and black – a plain administrative false-front; a veneer of the lifeless everyday that hid the sparkling humanity within.

This ingenious piece of furniture was what kept the Franks' presence secret for so long, but on 4 August 1944 the secret annex was raided by German uniformed police. The family were arrested, interrogated and then deported to Auschwitz concentration camp; Anne and her sister were later transferred to Bergen-Belsen camp, where they both died in early 1945. Anne was just fifteen years old.

The Franks were not alone in hiding from the Nazis during the Holocaust, and records reveal that many Jews were sheltered by friends, neighbours and others sympathetic to their plight – who housed them in attics and cellars, with entrances concealed by or within furniture.

The Polish Holocaust survivor Wilek Loew recounted his mother hiding inside a couch:

> A couch consisted of a frame and on top of the frame there was this soft part which is the couch. And you couldn't tell whether that couch was separate… for anyone else it was one part, the frame and the couch, the upper part, was one unit. That's why when there was any action, my mother will be hiding over there. I will make sure of that.

Similarly, Mirjam Geismar, a young Jewish girl living in the Netherlands, remembered being separated from her parents and having to go into hiding in a series of different people's houses. In one place she hid under the kitchen floor, accessed via a trapdoor, while her parents took refuge in Breeplein church in Rotterdam, where they lived in a special cupboard that had been built behind the church organ by the caretaker.

SHELTER DURING AIR RAIDS

In Britain, furniture helped to protect in another way: during air raids, when hiding under the kitchen table was quite common. David Smith, an eighty-eight-year-old retired schoolteacher from Exeter, remembers hiding under the dining-room table during air raids on London in 1940, but being told by his parents to get back into bed because it was too damp downstairs. Others remember owning reinforced steel-topped kitchen tables under which they sheltered. The Manchester-based auxiliary fireman Lancelot Helman spent an entire night during the war underneath the kitchen table, after he had arrived home from tending to a fire only to discover that a direct hit from a German bomb had levelled a nearby shelter, killing everyone inside it. There was very little that would protect you if a bomb landed right on top of where you were hiding.

A Morrison shelter, introduced in Britain in March 1941

To provide shelter outside the home, Anderson shelters – made out of galvanized corrugated steel, then dug into place and covered with earth – were supplied to almost 4 million homes immediately prior to and during the war. For indoor use, the Morrison shelter – named after its designer Herbert Morrison, and otherwise known as the 'Table Indoor Shelter' – was provided to more than half a million homes by the end of 1941.

Herbert Morrison (1888–1965)

Baron Morrison of Lambeth was a British Labour politician who acted as Home Secretary in the wartime coalition government, having previously held the post of Minister of Supply in 1940. He was a London councillor prior to his election to parliament in 1935, and this experience placed him well for dealing with the capital during the Blitz, as well as overseeing the design of the eponymous air shelter. After the war, he was involved in drafting the Labour party's election manifesto, and when his party won a landslide victory he was appointed deputy prime minister.

These shelters were made of wood and steel and came in assembly kits to be bolted together in the home. They measured 2 metres long by 1.2 metres wide and 0.75 metres high – roughly the size of a wardrobe on its back. They were built with a steel plate top and wire mesh down the sides, and came with a mattress on which the occupants would lie during an air raid. When not in use they functioned as a normal piece of household furniture – a dining-room or kitchen table – though some remember tap-dancing on the metal surface as young children, because of the sound that it made.

In his autobiography, Herbert Morrison recalled the story behind the shelter's invention. While the outdoor Anderson shelter was very safe, it was not suitable for homes with no garden and it was prone to flooding, which meant that an indoor solution needed to be found. The task was given to a team of scientists and engineers. Fearful that they would take ages arguing over the design, Morrison threatened to lock them in a room until they produced a plan – something that Churchill was rumoured to be delighted by. The design of the Morrison shelter was received less than twenty-four hours later.

And they were effective. In an examination after the Blitz by the Ministry of Home Security of some thirty-nine badly damaged houses in different parts of Britain – in which people had hidden under Morrison shelters during an air raid – only four fatalities were recorded, seven people were seriously injured and fourteen slightly. Fifty-four were uninjured. The majority remained unscathed, therefore, and the fatalities had occurred only in houses that suffered a direct hit.

STATE ECONOMIC PROTECTION

At the start of the war, the German bombing raids created an unexpected crisis. A lack of timber combined with an increased demand for new furniture from those who had lost their household possessions put unsustainable pressure on the furniture industry. Joan Styan later recalled the impact of the Blitz in London and the chaos it caused, with houses demolished or collapsed, and furniture leaning at bizarre angles from upstairs rooms. People lost everything and had to live without cupboards, chairs and tables, making do with whatever they could lay their hands on.

As a result, the entire furniture industry – from the sourcing of timber to the manufacture and consumption of products – was overseen by the government, with the aim of protecting it at a time of national emergency and shortage. In 1942, the Utility Furniture Advisory Committee was set up to take control of the situation, and they set about designing functional and robust furniture for the general population – which was first advertised in the *Utility Furniture Catalogue* of 1943.

The designers created strong, hard-wearing pieces of furniture that were without frills. The idea was to use as little wood as possible in order to make the most efficient use of timber (which was scarce), with little in the way of ornamentation or carvings. This minimalist aesthetic was in direct contrast to consumer tastes of the period, and as soon as restrictions were relaxed in the post-war years, people hankered after much more decorative furniture – although mid-century Utility furniture is much sought-after today.

In order to control supply, the government introduced strict furniture rationing, with new items being restricted to newly-weds and those who had been bombed out of their homes. This was legislated by the 'Domestic Furniture (Control of Manufacture and Supply (No 2)) Order 1942', which was operative from 1 November 1942. Later on, families with pregnant women or young children were given priority; not only did the government protect the furniture industry, therefore, but also the most vulnerable in their war-torn world – a powerful reminder of how important furniture was considered to be to the maintenance of a civilized society.

·10·

MOTHERS

—

The Cross of Honour of the German Mother, established
16 December 1938 and last awarded 8 May 1945

The history of mothers is all about shame...

A MOTHER'S MEDAL

Women were responsible not only for giving birth to the new members of the new Germany, but also for rearing and raising them as perfect citizens of the Nazi Reich. In 1934, six weeks after Hitler took power, the Nazi propaganda minister Josef Goebbels gave a speech at the opening of a women's exhibition in Berlin, and used the occasion to drive home a message about the importance of mothers to the state:

> Clear and often drastic examples will give thousands of German women reason to think and consider. It is particularly pleasing to us men in the new government that families with many children are given particular attention, since we want to rescue the nation from decline. The importance of the family cannot be overestimated...

As part of the drive to increase the German population, Hitler issued an order in December 1938 decreeing that it was the duty of all mothers to give birth to multiple children for the good of the Reich. As part of this push for progeny, mothers were to be awarded with a ceremonial cross, the Cross of Honour of the German Mother, in recognition of their service to the nation. The first ceremony took place on the following Mother's Day – 21 May 1939. Since 1920, a similar medal had been presented to French mothers of large families, the *Médaille de la Famille française*.

Women in Germany who gave birth to four children would receive a bronze cross; those who had six children were given silver; while those who brought up eight or more were rewarded for their remarkable efforts with a gold award. It is estimated that in this way more than 5 million women received a cross of some order. So powerful was this ideology of motherhood that women in Nazi Germany clamoured to be awarded the cross by officials, since it was a measure of their worth within society. Motherhood was nothing less than a service to the German nation, and to fail in one's duty – or even to be seen to fail – was met with censure and shame.

Josef Goebbels (1897–1945)

A gifted orator and strategist who was responsible for recruiting the masses to Nazism in the 1930s and painting a favourable picture of the Nazi regime for the German people throughout the war. He held the position of Reich Minister of Propaganda of Nazi Germany from 1933 to 1945 and was one of Hitler's closest supporters and allies. Rabidly anti-Semitic, he advocated for the extermination of the Jews. Goebbels joined the Nazi party in 1924, in its earliest days, and stayed until the very end. He was with Hitler in the bunker in Berlin when Hitler took his own life on 30 April 1945. Goebbels committed suicide with his wife the following day, and also poisoned all of his six children.

In recent years, hundreds of letters have come to light in the Berlin archives written by German mothers begging for recognition by the authorities for bringing children into the Nazi world. Women who gave birth to children with disabilities, who had relatives with criminal records, or who did not otherwise meet the Reich's exacting standards for the Aryan race were refused their reward. Such rejections could cause significant emotional distress. One of the most telling letters was addressed to Karl Kaufmann, the top Nazi official in Hamburg, in May 1941. It reads:

> Dear Gauleiter Kaufmann, have I been forgotten? I have had eight children and am now pregnant again. I have not received my Golden Cross. My mother-in-law says this is a great shame and my husband was violent towards me today because of this. Please help.

Another letter was from a mother of eleven, complaining of not receiving a cross she strongly felt that she deserved: 'We're really not criminals. Hereditary disease, prison, jail, alcohol abuse – these things do not exist in our family. I feel unworthy because I have not got the cross.'

UNMARRIED ENGLISH MOTHERS

In England, it was unmarried mothers who were shamed, as the Church and the national press rose together in moral outrage at the increase in illegitimate births created by the conflict. The Bishop of Norwich chastised 'women and especially young girls in town and village alike' for casual relationships with soldiers, warning:

> we are in danger of our national character rotting at the root... nothing is more alarming than the decay of personal standards of sexual morality... nothing threatens more the future of our race. When men and women grow loose in personal morality they endanger their own eternal salvation and they endanger too the England of tomorrow.

Statistically there was a shift in births of children outside of wedlock: 4.4 per cent of children in 1939 were born to unmarried mothers, compared with 9.18 per cent in 1945. The registrar general was of the view that the higher rate of pregnancies among young women did not reflect moral degeneracy, but was because of the 'enforced degree of physical separation of the sexes' caused by the war. The stationing of young men abroad had the effect of 'rendering immediate marriage with their home brides increasingly difficult – and, in the case of many quite impossible'. These were to his mind only temporary circumstances.

Some women became pregnant before they could marry men who were called up to fight, while a number of married, widowed or separated women fell pregnant by men other than their husbands. The blackouts were another consideration – they made unmarried women more vulnerable to unwanted sexual advances, and instances of rape explain some of the childbirths outside of marriage.

Whatever the explanation, the children of such women were deemed 'illegitimate', and the mothers received inadequate help from public services while also faced with families who could not – or would not – help. Some were evacuated in order to give birth away from the communities in which they had grown up, but many authorities in the areas in which these women arrived found unmarried mothers and their newborn offspring a burden on local finances, and so some women found themselves put on trains 'home' – back to where they had been brought up. There was an attempt by voluntary organizations and the government to place women in mother-and-baby homes, but this was fraught with difficulty, not least because the mothers themselves often preferred not to attend such harshly run institutions. For other women, their babies were hurriedly adopted – especially when the mother was married but the child was not that of the husband; but this happened in circumstances that did not put the welfare of either the child or mother first.

The personal experiences of individual unmarried mothers are revealing of the hardships they faced. Doreen Bates, for example, was a tax inspector who bore twins by a married colleague and then returned to work, only to be warned by her boss that she would be sacked if such a thing happened again. Other brave women who similarly challenged societal norms were duly dismissed by their employers.

It was within families, however, that perhaps the strictest censure came. A Mrs Needham from Lancashire remembered her mother's reaction to her falling pregnant by a young man from a different social background. When her family failed in their attempt to find the father and force him to marry their daughter, her mother responded with severity, forcing her into the workhouse 'because', according to Needham, 'she thought it was wrong what I had done'.

In other families, attempts were made to hide unwanted pregnancies from the rest of the world because of the sense of social stigma attached to the 'shame' of unmarried mothers. The rock star Eric Clapton, for example, was born in Surrey in 1945 to an unmarried sixteen-year-old girl who had become pregnant by a twenty-four-year-old Canadian serviceman, and was brought up by his grandparents – who he thought were his parents. It was not until he overheard his aunt and uncle referring to his real 'mum' and him as a 'little bastard' that the truth dawned on him that he was being brought up in a house full of secrets. When his biological mother visited his grandparents when he was nine, he asked if he could now call her mother, to which she replied 'No', and said that he should go on calling his grandparents Mum and Dad. The impact of this rejection was traumatic, and Clapton developed a close attachment to the family dog – and, later on, to music – all the while keeping up the pretence of the family secret.

THE MOTHERS' MOVEMENT

A fear of such unfettered and 'shameful' female sexual activity underlaid the philosophy of the 'mothers' movement', a collection of between 50 and 100 far-right women's groups in the United States that operated between 1939 and 1941. Groups like Chicago's

'We the Mothers Mobilize for America', 'Detroit's Mothers of the U.S.A.', and 'Cincinnati's Mothers of Sons Forum' were aligned with the America First Committee, a pressure group that advocated non-intervention in the war.

America First

'America First' was a slogan used by President Woodrow Wilson (1856–1924) at the beginning of the First World War, and then by President Warren G. Harding (1865–1923) during the 1920 election campaign. It represented a policy that emphasized US nationalism and unilateralism and sought to pursue an isolationist foreign policy in order to protect America's interests. It was adopted during the interwar period by the America First Committee.

The majority of women in the United States supported the war effort wholeheartedly: they took jobs in munitions factories, volunteered for military service, staffed government bureaucracy, served as nurses, and symbolized national unity and the strength of the nation. There were, however, a minority who – for a range of reasons connected to religion, maternal love and deep-seated prejudice – fundamentally opposed America's involvement in the war.

At the root of their concern as mothers was family; as with other American women, they feared that their sons and menfolk would be drafted into the army. The way that they interpreted this possibility, however, was different from the majority of mothers. What ultimately concerned them was an attack on the traditional core of family values, perpetuated by a government (bankrolled by international Jewish bankers) bent on world interventionism and continual global conflict – into which the male members of their families would inevitably be drawn. The upshot of this, they believed, would be the erosion of the patriarchal family, the rise of maternally headed households and the proliferation of shameful sexual immorality. For these women, the war was nothing less than an attack on their fundamentalist Christian values.

In this context, the rhetoric of motherhood and maternal care masked some pretty dramatic campaigning. On 22 August 1940, a coalition of groups calling themselves the Congress of American Mothers gathered outside the Capitol Building in Washington, DC, to protest the Roosevelt administration's financial aid to the British and peacetime conscription. And in the same month, the Mothers of the U.S.A. paraded against Senator Claude Pepper of Florida – a supporter of these policies – by hanging an effigy of him from a tree and chanting 'We'll hang Claude Pepper to a sour apple tree.'

Elizabeth Dilling (1894–1966)

A prominent right-wing female activist during the 1930s who was an outspoken critic of the New Deal, the series of public programmes and projects aimed at stimulating the US economy after the Great Depression. Dilling was one of the best-known leaders of the women's isolationist movement during the Second World War, and sought to pressure Congress to refrain from assisting the Allies in the war.

After America entered the war, such tactics were tantamount to treason, and members of the mothers' movement such as Elizabeth Dilling were called to testify before a Grand Jury in

1944 at what became known as 'the Great Sedition Trial'. This case saw a number of individuals tried for violating US sedition laws and being pro-Nazi conspirators. But these women – in their own minds, at least – had simply protested in order to keep their families free of 'shame'.

·11·
PUPPETS

Papier mâché puppet of a Jewish man in a prison uniform

Puppets are all about totalitarian rule
and the struggle for freedom...

Puppets have been a powerful metaphor for totalitarian rule for millennia. Puppeteers, both serious and playful, have consistently explored twin themes that are constantly in tension with each other: the total control of one being by another and the desire to break free. It is not surprising, therefore, that puppetry appears time and again in the history of the Second World War – in this era of absolute control and a global struggle for freedom.

PUPPETS OF JEWS

The United States Holocaust Memorial Museum in Washington, DC, has an astonishing collection of puppets, which includes examples from a collection of 900 objects brought together by Peter Ehrenthal, a survivor of the Holocaust in Romania. Ehrenthal amassed these objects with one specific purpose: to reveal the depth and pervasiveness of anti-Semitism in Western culture throughout history.

The collection includes posters, paintings, decorative art, toys and everyday household items, each portraying a stereotypical representation of a Jew. One item is a papier mâché puppet used in an unknown show. The puppet is of a balding man whose bare skull is covered by a smart black Jewish cap – the traditional kippah; he wears tightly fitting round glasses, has a large nose and his fine clothes are distinctively Jewish in their geometric pattern and cut. So far, so unremarkable: puppets with exaggerated and cartoon-like features were common. What makes this puppet stand out, however, is that it *squeaks* when the stomach is pressed or squashed or perhaps even struck – a telling reminder of how a Jewish puppet might be treated in a show. Particularly revealing is the fact that the curators do not know when this puppet is from. So pervasive was anti-Semitism expressed for public consumption that they believe the puppet could have been made and used at any time between 1800 and 1901. Such foundations of hatred give context to how Nazi anti-Semitism was accepted by so many in the 1930s and 1940s throughout Eastern Europe.

The Holocaust in Romania

Between 1941 and 1944, under the leadership of its military dictator, Marshal Ion Antonescu, Romania executed around 300,000 Jews – approximately 50 per cent of its Jewish population. In a direct echo of Nazi policy, the programme was undertaken to 'purify' the Romanian nation. The Romanian army conducted mass shootings, and thousands more died from starvation and epidemic in forced resettlement programmes. Romania maintained its independence during the war, but it was allied with Germany in its war against Russia and gave Germany access to its immense supplies of crude oil.

The collection contains another puppet of a Jew, but this one is worlds apart from the earlier example. It too is of a man, but this time the glasses have gone. This man peers out at the audience with dark rings around his sunken eyes. His smart kippah has been replaced by something ill-fitting and ill-made. His expensive patterned clothes have gone, now replaced by a dark green, rough wool akin to sackcloth. Across the stomach, presumably holding up the trousers on what would be a thin skeleton, is a simple piece of string as a belt.

This puppet is also a stereotype, but it depicts a newer type of Jew – one that had been created by the Nazis: this is the puppet of an *incarcerated* Jew. Unlike the earlier puppet, which could have been made at almost any point across an entire century, curators are quite certain that this puppet was made at a very specific time, when the appearance of an entire people was altered in the process of attempting to eradicate them: 1941–4. These puppets may be mute, but they still speak eloquently to us, across the ages, of a history of dominance and hatred.

CZECH RESISTANCE

In the same period, however, puppets were also used to convey exactly the opposite meaning; they were about escape, defiance and resistance against the puppetmaster, the person who represented total control. One of the most common themes in puppet theatre is subversion, achieved through guile and artlessness – or simply through confrontation and unruliness. And such subversion is a most effective way of making dictatorship appear ludicrous. As a result, puppetry has consistently flourished as a tool of resistance in times of democratic crisis, and this was no less so in World War Two.

Puppetry flourished in particular in Czechoslovakia, where there was already a long-established tradition of outspoken and radical puppetry. When European countries fell under Nazi rule, it was common for the local population to fall back on traditional cultural practices as a way of maintaining their identity. One way this manifested itself in Czechoslovakia was through puppet shows, which provided Czechs with a way of identifying with and promoting their heritage while at the same time creating a perfect platform for subverting the new regime. The pure entertainment value of the puppet shows, meanwhile, helped to ease the anxieties and social tensions that arose from occupation.

Improvised puppet shows flourished in secret – in bars and basements. These shows became known as 'daisies', and the name was carefully chosen. Daisies flower in the most inhospitable of conditions: they push up through cracks; they flower amid the gloom. And putting on these shows was a dangerous business. More than 100 Czech puppeteers are believed to have been killed in concentration camps, incarcerated for criticizing the new regime.

German-occupied Czechslovakia

Germany broke up Czechoslovakia in 1939, and occupied much of its territory during the war. The Germans absorbed the significant Czech army into their forces, and adapted its armaments factories to make German-designed aircraft, tanks and artillery. But the Czech resistance was responsible for one of the biggest insurgency successes of the entire war – the assassination of Reinhard Heydrich (see p. 63) – and felt the full brunt of Hitler's wrath in retaliation when he ordered the arrest and execution of 10,000 randomly selected Czechs, as well as the complete destruction of two entire Czech villages, Lidice and Ležáky.

GREEK MOUNTAIN FIGHTERS

Resistance theatre during the war was also seen in Greece, where it worked in a different way – by bringing political ideas to peasants in mountain villages who had little exposure to news or opinion concerning contemporary events, but who had a particular affinity with traditional, oral folk culture. Wild areas with poor education and low literacy were no place for written mani-festos, and yet the need to transmit the message of resistance to the rural population was urgent.

Those who put on the plays in the early years of the war were not professional performers but *andartes* – the mountain fighters of the Greek Resistance. These men used performances effectively to spread their message, to crow of their deeds, and to cultivate allies in the remote areas in which they needed to operate.

The Greek Resistance

In October 1940, Italy declared war on Greece but was soon forced into a stalemate; this deadlock was dramatically broken in April 1941, when the Germans attacked and swiftly occupied the country. Greece has a long tradition of resistance fighters going back to the Fall of Constantinople in 1453, after which large areas of the country came under Ottoman control. Under German occupation, the folk-hero status of Greece's mountain-dwelling resistance fighters was revived. Opposition to German occupation was immediate, and the insurgents organized into three politically distinct resistance groups: ELAS, EDES and EKKA. The sub-sequent rivalry between these groups was one of the prime causes of the Greek Civil War (1946-9).

As the weight of war fell fully upon Greece, however, groups of professional performers gathered in the mountains, performing to adults in return for food and to children for free. One typical troupe proclaimed its arrival in a village from the top of the church's bell tower, announcing: 'The ticket for all is from one oka wheat, or two oka potatoes, or onions, or hazel nuts, or oil, the equivalent of each thing to one oka wheat. No one can enter without a ticket.'

Puppeteers were common among such performers. Not only did they entertain and teach about resistance and liberty through songs and shows, but they instructed the young and willing how to become puppeteers themselves. Such self-awareness of the value of puppetry in helping to grow networks of resistance was one of the most important reasons for its sustained role in – and impact on – the Second World War.

·12·
COWS

VRVS SVM, POLONIS TVR, GERMANIS AVROX:
IGNARI BISONTIS NOMEN DEDERANT

Illustration of an aurochs from Sigismund von Herberstein's
Rerum Moscoviticarum Comentarii (1556)

Cows are all about technological innovation...

NAZI SUPER COWS

In the 1920s in Weimar Germany, two brothers – Lutz and Heinz Heck, sons of the director of the Berlin Zoo – began a series of experiments to genetically reverse-engineer a breed of animal that went extinct in 1627: the aurochs, a large, horned cattle that was hunted out of existence. The pair believed that they could recreate these beasts by combining contemporary specimens that possessed the right traits in terms of size, colour, horns and temperament – including aggressive Spanish bulls. The resulting breed was reared not in order to feed a growing and militarized German population but as part of the ideological and romantic German vision of *Lebensraum*, the territory and space that the Nazis saw as necessary for the natural development of their Aryan nation.

Lebensraum

The German concept of *Lebensraum* (which literally translates as 'living space') dates back to the 1890s, and is connected to German colonialization. *Lebensraum* was a key geopolitical goal of Imperial Germany during the First World War – as part of the *Septemberprogramm* of territorial expansion. It was with the Nazis, however, that it was developed most fully – as a key ideological principle that justified German expansion in Europe.

The Heck brothers' experiments on resurrecting extinct animals from Germany's past were based on a process known as 'back-breeding'. In this period – which was before the discovery of DNA in the 1950s – this time-consuming work was fundamentally historical, and involved trawling through written records and studying archaeological finds such as skulls and cave paintings to build a picture of the physical characteristics of extinct breeds like the German wisent (or European bison) and the mighty aurochs. As Lutz put it in his autobiography, *Animals: My Adventure* (1954): 'What my brother and I now had to do was to unite in a single breeding stock all those characteristics of the wild animal which are now found only separately in individual animals.'

Lutz Heck joined the Nazi party in June 1933, and with its patronage he succeeded in creating something similar to the aurochs, now known as 'Heck cattle', by the mid-1930s. These specimens were tall, with large horns and aggressive personalities, they could withstand long cold winters on hard ground and required almost no care from humans in order to survive. The breed still exists today, and has drawn headlines in the UK around concerns over introducing such aggressive livestock into Devon.

In seeking to bring back primeval Germanic beasts from the nation's mythical past, Lutz Heck's scientific fascination merged with a Nazi desire to recreate and repopulate what were seen as long-lost landscapes. His work thus found parallels in the Nazi desire for racial purity, and the *Generalplan Ost*, Heinrich Himmler's plan to 'restore' territory in Central and Eastern Europe to Germany as part of the envisioned *Lebensraum*.

The engineered aurochs fitted into this grand scheme in a rather expansive way, and were allowed to run rampant through the forest areas of this 'restored' land, including the Białowieża Forest which borders Poland and Belarus. They were introduced along with moose, bears and lynx, and were game for hunting, a popular pastime among the Nazi elite. Heck joined in – now killing the animals he had created – along with his hunting companions, including Hermann Göring, one of the most powerful figures in the Nazi party. In this, both Göring and Heck were inspired by the medieval epic poem *Nibelungenlied*, in which forest-dwelling Teutonic knights hunted deer, boar and aurochs. This souped-up Nazi cow was therefore closely connected to Nazi ideology – and a lost mythology of the aristocratic hunter.

MILKING AND ANTIBIOTICS

In wartime America – with an ever-greater demand for foodstuffs in order to feed their own troops, their home population and to help out almost all Allied countries with the exception of China – the livestock industry introduced a whole series of technological advances to guarantee the supply of cows for meat and milk.

During the early 1940s, the number of cattle in farms throughout the country soared to an all-time high, rising from 68.4 million in 1940 to more than 85.6 million in the final year of the war. The way that cattle were raised and fattened was revolutionized during this period. One of the key practical innovations saw livestock confined in large feedlots (which were designed to cater for large herds) and fattened scientifically. Among the most concentrated and intensive feedlots in the US during these years were in south-west Kansas and the Texas and neighbouring Oklahoma panhandles.

The aim of these new feeding regimes was to breed resistance into cattle and inoculate them from the kinds of diseases that might previously have decimated a farmer's entire stock. This meant the introduction of new antibiotics to the feed. One such super-drug prescribed to cattle was streptomycin, which had been pioneered in 1943 by Selman Waksman, the New Jersey-based microbiologist. It is claimed that this drug was responsible for wiping out bovine tuberculosis. Additives were also put into livestock feed in order to bulk them out during shortages of feed crops during wartime

– including urea, which was added in large quantities as it was manufactured synthetically and quite cheaply.

These new developments in the meat industry were paralleled by technological advances in milk production. The introduction of machinery and automated techniques modernized the American dairy industry, and milk cans, buckets and traditional stools were replaced by tanks and pumps that increased milk yields and milking speeds. In 1944, the number of dairy cows in the US peaked at some 25.6 million animals, each producing around 4,572 pounds of milk per year.

Selman Waksman (1888–1973)

One of the most important medical scientists in history. A Ukrainian-born, Jewish-American professor of biochemistry and microbiology at Rutgers University in New Jersey, he discovered numerous antibiotics and his work led to the discovery of many more. He set up the Waksman Institute of Microbiology from the money that flowed in from his many patents, and in 1952 he was awarded the Nobel Prize in Physiology or Medicine for his discovery of the antibiotic streptomycin.

BULLY BEEF

War has for a long time been seen as a catalytic force for accelerating technological change, and this crucible-like impact extended to the processes of food preservation – in particular the canning of food in order to extend its shelf life.

The Second World War saw a dramatic increase in canned products, not least salted corned beef. And the production of corned beef for the Allies was dominated by one company alone

– Fray Bentos, whose factory was located some 180 miles up the Uruguay River from Buenos Aires. Originally this had been a beef processing plant, set up in 1866 by the German chemist Justus von Liebig to produce a meat extract that came to be known as 'Oxo'. The company passed into British ownership, and during 1943 they exported over 16 million cans of corned beef alone.

The beef they produced was cheap, easy to carry, long-lasting and nutritious – a perfect diet for wartime. It became a staple ration for front-line troops and was colloquially known as 'bully beef'. Corporal Bill Cheall, who was with the Green Howards of the 50th Division at Dunkirk, remembers not having had a hot meal 'for God knows how long' and surviving on a ration diet of 'hard tack biscuits and bully beef'. Another soldier, Corporal John Dukes of the Royal Army Service Corps, wrote in his diary joking of the monotony of the food: 'I knew then that it would be bully for dinner, tea and supper. In fact, we have eaten that much bully, instead of walking now – we gallop!'

The experience of soldiers during the wars did much to popularize canned food for a domestic market too. At a time when fresh meat was strictly rationed in Britain, the Ministry of Food sought to educate home cooks in the gastronomic delights of canned corned beef, with recipes for corned beef hash and corned beef and oatmeal pudding.

Remains of the technology that provided those cans survive today in the Fray Bentos Industrial Landscape, a UNESCO World Heritage site since 2015. The rambling and haunting industrial complex is built on land projecting into the Uruguay River, and has its origins in a factory built to process the meat that was farmed on the endless prairies nearby. The company claimed that it used every part of the cow 'except for the Moo'.

The quality of the plant's historical remains is outstanding: the cavernous cold-storage building that could hold 18,000 tonnes of frozen meat; the engine room, the water tower and the tall brick chimney for the boiler; the killing room, where as many as 1,600 animals were slaughtered a day, still complete with its hooks, pulleys, chains, wheels and scales. Inside the engine room are generators, turbines, levers, valves, wheels, pipes, chimneys, dials and switches. The Casa Grande (the manager's house) also survives – an opulent mansion of hardwood floors and stained glass windows – as do some 300 homes built for the senior staff. Visitors can also see parts of the port facilities, from where the beef was shipped around the world – a lifeline which ran from this small corner of South America across thousands of miles to battlefronts and civilian kitchens all over Europe, North Africa and the Pacific. It is indisputably one of the most important technological and industrial sites of the war. And it is somewhat ironic that the Fray Bentos factory was a fundamental reason that the Second World War was even possible – in the 1860s when it was first set up, it was run by Germans and financed by the British.

·13·

HANDKERCHIEFS

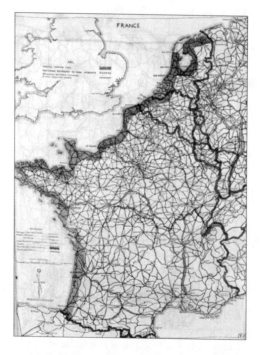

Silk escape map carried by Group Captain Hugh Beresford Verity when flying
over France and Germany with No. 161 Squadron RAF

The handkerchief is all about resistance…

ESCAPE MAPS

Throughout the course of the war, an estimated 1.75 million silk or rayon maps – some of them in the form of handkerchiefs – were manufactured for British forces in order to facilitate their escape if they went down behind enemy lines or were imprisoned in POW camps. A symbol of dogged determination, the handkerchief map demonstrated how attitudes towards being captured had changed since the First World War, when imprisonment was viewed with a sense of failure and shame. During the Second World War, military command sought to encourage a positive outlook of 'escape-mindedness'. Concentrating the troops on trying to escape was a way of instilling a sense of mission among prisoners and raising their morale, as well as an effective means of tying up enemy manpower and resources to prevent escapes, thus keeping valuable soldiers from the front lines. The handkerchief map, therefore, represented a form of resistance that existed inside prison camps.

The department behind the manufacture of these maps was MI9. As MI9's chief technical officer – a bit like the character Q from *James Bond* – Christopher Clayton Hutton masterminded the mapping programme. Silk maps were at the very heart of his strategy; he considered them to be 'the escapee's most important accessory'. Hutton used silk because it was lightweight yet strong, and folded up easily and silently – unlike paper, which crumples, tears and rustles.

The maps were made using commercially available maps of Europe, the Middle East and North Africa, produced by the Edinburgh-based company John Bartholomew & Son Ltd. Bartholomew waived copyright of the maps in order to assist the war effort. They were reproduced at a greatly reduced scale – from 1:250,000 to 1:5000,000, a quarter of the size produced on paper. Despite their diminutive size, some of them measuring just 25cm by 19cm, the font and print were perfectly legible and the detail was dense but readable.

An example of a silk map intended to be stuffed into a pocket survives today in the collections of the Imperial War Museum in London. Made of silk and measuring 57cm by 42cm, this map belonged to Group Captain Hugh Beresford Verity, who served in No. 161 Squadron RAF, a highly secretive unit of the Royal Air Force that often worked with Britain's two clandestine military branches, the Special Operations Executive (SOE) and the Secret Intelligence Service (SIS). Verity frequently found himself flying over enemy territory in the 118 sorties that he made. On one side of the fabric is a map of France, and on the other a map of Germany. It is typical of the sorts of silk maps that were routinely provided for such flight personnel.

MI9

Section 9 of the British Directorate of Military Intelligence (MI9) was founded on 23 December 1939, with the aim of facilitating the escape of British prisoners of war. Working with European resistance groups, MI9 agents sought to free airmen downed in enemy territory as well as POWs in prison camps in occupied Europe.

HANDKERCHIEF SMUGGLING

Production of these handkerchief escape maps raised the important question of how to disseminate them to those in prison. The solution was to smuggle them in, and this was done in a number of ways. MI9 worked with the makers of board games, gramophone records and even cricket bats to design ways of concealing maps during the manufacturing process. One of the key companies who cooperated was John Waddington Ltd, famed for the board game Monopoly. Wartime sets of the game contained maps concealed within the board itself, and genuine foreign currency was put among the Monopoly money in order to assist prisoners during their escape. Maps were also concealed inside chess sets, printed on playing cards and secreted in gramophone records, which needed to be smashed to reveal the map – a practice that was jokingly nicknamed 'Operation Smash Hit'.

Parcels of provisions for prisoners sent by fictitious agencies such as the Ladies Knitting Circle, The Jigsaw Club and the Prisoners' Leisure Hour Club were used to smuggle silk maps. And these parcels provided opportunities for the exchange of secret correspondence, as the Germans obligingly allowed prisoners to send home a receipt saying that they had received a package safely. By December 1941 there was a network of over 900 secret code letter-writers operating out of POW camps and communicating with MI9 operatives. An estimated 100 letters made their way in and out of the camps each month. In this manner, MI9 were able to keep open effective channels of communication that directly facilitated the escape of prisoners.

ESCAPE FROM COLDITZ

It is likely that Airey Neave, the first British officer to escape from the legendary German prison fortress Colditz,* planned his escape route using a miniature handkerchief map covering Germany and northern Switzerland. Neave's own account of his escape can be found in his memoir *They Have Their Exits* (1953),

---

* Rather than Pat Reid, as claimed in the film *The Colditz Story* (1955).

and is deliberately evasive on the techniques and materials used. The book was published just eight years after the end of the war, when the restrictions regarding the public disclosure of MI9's methodology would still have been active. However, historians believe that Neave was working with a map received from London in one of the many packages containing escape materials that War Office accounts in the National Archives prove were sent to Colditz before January 1941.

Airey Neave (1916–79)

Airey Middleton Sheffield Neave was a British soldier, lawyer and MP who was imprisoned in and then escaped from Colditz. Educated at Eton and Merton College, Oxford, Neave served in the territorial army, and transferred to the Royal Engineers in 1938. On 23 May 1940 he was wounded and captured by the Germans while serving with the Searchlight Regiment, Royal Artillery. He was imprisoned and escaped from prison in Thorn in April 1941, and subsequently captured and sent to Colditz. On arrival home he was awarded the Military Cross, and was recruited to work for MI9 as an intelligence agent. He later served as an MP, and was blown up by an INLA bomb attack on the Houses of Parliament in 1979.

Neave's route took him by foot and train from Leisnig and Leipzig and then on to Singen, to cross the Swiss border not at its nearest point but at the Schaffhausen Salient, which protrudes into German territory. Travelling this route they avoided the eastern end of Lake Constance, which was the naturally shorter and more obvious passage but was more heavily patrolled. Nine months later, Captain Pat Reid of the Royal Army Service Corps and Flight Lieutenant H. N. Wardle of the RAF escaped following an identical route, confirming that there was an accurate map and an effective map-supply system in place for would-be escapees.

To safeguard maps that had successfully made it into locations like Colditz and make sure that they were able to be used by others, those planning an escape were required to make their own copies and memorize their route. Control over the handling of these handkerchief maps in camps was tight. An escape committee took responsibility for all planned escapes, approving those they believed workable, and one of the members was appointed map officer – whose responsibility it was to hide such maps. Neave carefully describes in his account how he made a copy of a map in 'Indian ink'. It is likely, therefore, that Reid and Neave did not just base their escape routes on similar maps, but on the exact same one. Historians now believe this to have been one of two maps of the Schaffhausen Salient.

By the end of the war, more than 36,000 British men had made their way home having been shot down behind enemy lines, evaded capture or escaped from camps – and silk handkerchief maps played a key role in helping them navigate their way out of enemy territory into neutral countries, and to eventually find their way home.

CODE BOOKS

Silk escape maps were not the only form of handkerchief resistance in the war. Their size and material also made them perfect for recording codes. In the summer of 1944, small teams known as 'Jedburghs' were inserted into occupied France, Belgium and the Netherlands to provide assistance to resistance fighters. They all received specialized training in guerrilla warfare and equipment designed for clandestine operations and unconventional warfare. One of the most important pieces of equipment was their field radio, which weighed just nine pounds but had a range of 500 miles. The messages were encoded using a silk handkerchief just 23cm by 11.5cm in size, on which were printed 500 four-letter codes chosen specifically for requesting or reporting operations.

Using this kit, these teams pioneered techniques that are still used by special forces today – and the silk handkerchiefs were a distinctive feature. One British soldier, Sergeant Arthur Wood – who took part in Operation Houndsworth, an SAS operation in the summer of 1944 that aided the French Resistance in Dijon and Burgundy – clearly recalled the inconvenience of having to encode and decode all messages sent and received, a time-consuming and onerous task in which two men operated the wireless and two more took responsibility for the coding. Recalling his service on BBC Radio Norfolk in 2005, Wood proudly noted that he still had in his possession the handkerchief code book that had been so important to the success of his operation, a physical manifestation of the resistance that helped turn the war in France – in the form of a silk handkerchief.

·14·

PAPERBACKS

Armed Services Edition of *The Great Gatsby*

Paperbacks are all about freedom...

During the Second World War, publishers in America gave away 122,951,031 paperback books to troops fighting all over the world. It was an impressive logistical achievement as well as a magnificent demonstration of philanthropy. In doing so, they transformed the publishing industry and inspired an entire generation to read and admire books.

BOOK BURNING

In 1933, the Nazis staged public book burnings designed to 'cleanse' the German spirit of un-German thoughts and ideas – essentially those that were communist, pacifist or penned by Jewish authors. The burnings took place in thirty-four university towns across Germany, and were met with widespread support and reporting from the German media. Persecuted authors included some of the most famous names in literature: Karl Marx, Albert Einstein, Ernst Bloch, Victor Hugo, James Joyce, Aldous Huxley and D. H. Lawrence.

These German burnings were also well-reported in the press and newsreels across America, where they were viewed with horror for the ruthless way in which the Nazi authorities sought to police thought. Demonstrations took place in dozens of cities across America, and the burnings were condemned by nearly all US newspapers. The famous critic Ludwig Lewisohn (1882–1955) who wrote for *The Nation*, one of the most influential publications of the day, saw in the Nazi book burnings a terrible promise. He wrote of how it forecast a 'dark age', and that it was an assault 'against the life of the mind, intellectual values, and the rights of the human spirit'. *Newsweek* even used the term 'holocaust' in their description of the book-burning campaign.

Erich Kästner (1899–1974), the German author of the internationally famous children's book *Emil and the Detectives* (1929), witnessed first-hand the burning that took place at the Opernplatz in Berlin. He later wrote:

> I stood in front of the university, wedged between students
> in SA uniforms, in the prime of their lives, and saw our
> books flying into the quivering flames... it was disgusting.

A WAR OF IDEAS

A decade later, and with America now in the war after the surprise Japanese bombing of Pearl Harbor, the US publishing industry mobilized books as weapons of war. The people behind the movement were a group of publishers, booksellers, authors, librarians and others with an interest in the book trade, who in 1942 formed the Council on Books in Wartime. This was their professional response to the cultural need to be seen to *do* something in support of the war effort. The council adopted the motto 'Books Are Weapons in the War of Ideas' and set about rallying their industry and their formidable network of contacts that reached far across America – as far as President Roosevelt himself – to help. Their subsequent achievements astonished everyone.

One of the first things that they did was to harness the propaganda power of the Nazi book burnings, as 1943 was the tenth anniversary. The council deliberately positioned themselves as the diametrical opposite of book-burners, a point most powerfully made in a poster from that year. This rectangular poster was divided by a diagonal line running from top right to bottom left. The top section was inhabited by a group of Nazi soldiers standing around a pile of burning books and making the Nazi salute, mouths open, chins stretching the straps on their distinctive Nazi kepis (caps). The space below the line, on the other hand, contained the Statue of Liberty, her hand also raised. She was holding up a torch – not to set fire to books, but to light the path to freedom – and she was crowned with the radiant halo of the cherished and the divine. The burning of books was thus presented as the antithesis of freedom; Germany as the antithesis of America.

Other posters made similar and powerful points. One which showed an evil-looking Hitler looming above a pile of burning books carried the message:

> He burns books because he is afraid of them. He knows good books are weapons of free men against the laws of the jungle which he must follow in his insane and ignorant effort to plunder and befoul the world.

Along with the publication of posters like this, the council organized a fully coordinated media blitz that included a radio dramatization of the Pulitzer Prize-winning American poet Stephen Vincent Benét's *They Burned the Books* (1942).

> Nine! Nine iron years of terror and evil!
> Nine years since a fire was lighted in a public square, in Berlin.
> Nine years since the burning of the books! Do you remember?
> Write it down in your calendars, May 10th, 1933,
> And write it down in red by the light of fire.

The listener is asked, 'Why bother about books?' After all:

> A book's a book. It's paper, ink and print.
> If you stab it, it won't bleed.

If you beat it, it won't bruise.
If you burn it, it won't scream.

The answer is that, through the burning of books, the Nazis:

... foul the present and the past,
Shut the mouth so that it cannot speak
Because it spoke of freedom.

Numerous examples of Nazi atrocity, unfairness and abuse follow in the verses before Benét delivers the lines that bring it all together:

They burned the books and that was the beginning.
We didn't know it then. We know it now.

The burning was also mentioned in newsreels, radio news programmes, talk shows, and newspaper and magazine columns. Eleanor Roosevelt (1884–1962) wrote on the book burnings in her hugely popular column 'My Day'. Her husband, the president, even got in on the act – with a powerful message printed on an Office of War Information poster:

Books cannot be killed by fire. People die, but books never die. No man and no force can put thought in a concentration camp forever. No man and no force can take from the world the books that embody man's eternal fight against tyranny. In this war, we know, books are weapons.

Such impressive words were evidence of the immense influence of the publishing industry in the United States at the time; but the Council on Books in Wartime also put its money on the table, and combined actions with their words.

'My Day'

Eleanor Roosevelt, First Lady of the United States, published a newspaper column six days a week between 1935 and 1962 that was syndicated to ninety newspapers, all over the country. Her audience was slightly over 4 million. The column covered who she met, where she went and what she thought. It became a political platform as well as a diary, and is an exceptional historical source. She was not a private diarist, and so 'My Day' is the only day-to-day account we have of her life.

A NEW WAY OF READING

From October 1943 the Council on Books in Wartime began to distribute the printed books for the armed forces, and they did so in a revolutionary way. Until this time, most books were hardbacks. But these were expensive and difficult to access; a commodity for a specific and wealthy clientele. The council set about changing this by using magazine presses to print books as cheaply as they could. They would print two copies of a book page on a single magazine page and then cut it in half, producing paperback books that were wider than they were tall and which would fit perfectly in the pocket of a military uniform. They were called the 'Armed Services Editions'.

These books were then shipped over the world, to wherever the military were serving. They were a carefully chosen mixture of genres and styles, including classics, contemporary bestsellers, biography, drama, poetry, fantasy, action, religion and science – and even self-help and educational titles such as Edward Kasner and James R. Newman's *Mathematics and the Imagination* (1940) and Robert Goffin's history *Jazz from the Congo to the Metropolitan* (1943). In all, 1,322 titles were published, all sold to the army at the cost of manufacture.

The principle behind the movement was eloquently captured in an editorial in the *New York Times* in June 1944:

> People of the Axis Lands are prevented by force from knowing the facts of the time, and are told what to think… People of this free nation are supplied with the truth as free men see it and are confidently left to think for themselves.

The military audience for these books was ravenous for the knowledge and stories they contained. Men and women who would not otherwise read took up books; those who were already readers found titles they would never have come across before; plots and characters became the focus of conversation; people read books in locations where English-language books had never been seen before.

FAN MAIL

The extraordinary value of these new books is revealed in the council's archives. In some cases, the authors received *thousands* of letters from servicemen and women all over the world. One of the most popular titles was Betty Smith's *A Tree Grows in Brooklyn* (1943), an inspirational semi-autobiographical novel about a young girl living in Brooklyn in the first two decades of the twentieth century, the main theme of which was the determination to rise above overpoweringly difficult circumstances. One reader wrote to Betty:

> As I write this, my heart cries out with joy and gratitude for the beautiful story that I know you wrote for me. I can't explain it but your story restored to me my faith in a

Supreme Deity. A surge of confidence has swept through me and I feel that maybe a fellow has a fighting chance in this world after all… I'm not ashamed of but instead extremely proud of the tears that have rolled down my cheeks as I reread the story I have learned to love.

Experiences like this were shared thousands of times over. This immense publication project was a triumph for freedom – the freedom to share ideas and the freedom to learn. It profoundly influenced the experience of war for those who fought – and, by demonstrating the market value of small, disposable paperback books, changed forever the way that books were created and consumed.

·15·
GATES

Postage stamp commemorating the tenth anniversary of Hitler's
rise to power, depicting the Brandenburg Gate

Gates are all about empire...

NAZI VICTORY

The Brandenburg Gate (in German, *Brandenburger Tor*) in Berlin had long been a significant site for the German military, and during the Second World War it was utilized by the Nazis for the celebration of territorial expansion and empire and to mark important occasions in the history and development of the Nazi party. Built in the eighteenth century at the instigation of Frederick William II, King of Prussia from 1786 to 1797, the gate occupies a central place in the heart of Berlin – close to the Reichstag building and at the western end of the long tree-lined boulevard Unter den Linden. The neoclassical iconography in the gate's design borrows from Greek mythology and shows the Athenian battle between the Lapiths and the Centaurs, which represents the victory of men over beasts – a theme that appealed to the Nazi ideals of national purity and empire. Draped in the red flags of the party, the Brandenburg Gate became an important symbol for the Nazis.

On the occasion of the Nazi seizure of power on 30 January 1933, a torchlit procession of thousands of uniformed Brownshirts, Stormtroopers and SS paramilitary members passed through the gate as a coordinated propaganda exercise designed to demonstrate Nazi power. Ten years later, the commemoration of a decade of Nazi rule saw the issuing of a stamp featuring a German eagle and swastika ascendant over the iconic gate.

In 1939, the gate formed the backdrop to two significant events. On 20 April, German troops paraded through the gate as part of Hitler's fiftieth birthday celebrations, and that autumn another display was put on – this time to celebrate the German military victories in Poland and the annexation of large parts of the country in the Molotov–Ribbentrop Pact. Once again, soldiers marched along Unter den Linden and under the Brandenburg Gate to demonstrate the might of the Nazi empire.

Hitler saluting in front of the Brandenburg Gate on the occasion of his fiftieth birthday celebrations

At the end of the war in Europe, as Berlin was reduced to rubble, it was on top of the Brandenburg Gate that the Soviet troops chose to plant their national flag, a mark of their victory over the German Reich. The gate continued to play an important symbolic role – especially during the Cold War and the revolutions of 1989, when, in contrast with its previous associations with the totalitarian regime, it became associated with freedom and unity.

Molotov–Ribbentrop Pact

Also known as the 'Nazi–Soviet Pact', this treaty of non-aggression was signed by Nazi Germany and the Soviet Union on 23 August 1939. It was a pact of neutrality after the invasion of Poland, and divided that country and surrounding territories of Lithuania, Latvia, Estonia, Finland and Romania into opposing spheres of Russian and German influence, with the new border being set along the Curzon Line. The treaty was severely criticized by other Allied powers, and the *Evening Standard* published a famous cartoon depicting Hitler greeting Stalin as 'The scum of the earth, I believe?' and Stalin replying: 'The bloody assassin of the workers, I presume?'

THE ARC DE TRIOMPHE

For the French, the Arc de Triomphe in Paris was an emblem of empire and military victory. Built between 1806 and 1836 in the middle of Place Charles de Gaulle and at the very top of the grandiose, tree-lined Champs-Élysées, this archway was originally a memorial to those who had lost their lives fighting for France during the French Revolutionary and Napoleonic wars. It became central to France's sense of its military past, and as such it was the focus of martial pageantry, celebration and memory – most notably during the annual Bastille Day parade, which sees troops processing down the Champs-Élysées in full ceremonial dress. Inscribed on the monument are the names of French victories and well-known generals, and directly underneath is the Tomb of the Unknown Soldier, commemorating the fallen during the Great War of 1914–18. After the interment of the soldier on Armistice Day 1920, all parades were routed around rather than through the gates, in honour of the soldier buried beneath the vault and all the dead that he represents.

With such cultural significance for the French, the Arc de Triomphe naturally became a focus for France's enemies. After the German victory over the French in the Franco-Prussian War in 1871, Kaiser Wilhelm I paraded his troops under the triumphal arch and down the Champs-Élysées. In 1940 the Nazis were quick to follow the kaiser's example, by marching troops through the French capital to commemorate the fall of France – with the arch serving as the backdrop. In both cases, the Germans used the arch to celebrate military victory and the extension of territorial empire.

After the liberation of Paris in August 1944, the Arc de Triomphe yet again formed the backdrop for pomp and celebration – this time as French and US armoured vehicles rolled down the Champs-Élysées and American airplanes flew overhead. And finally, when the war ended in 1945, the Arc de Triomphe appeared on an American stamp commemorating the American success in the war, just as the Brandenburg Gate had appeared on German stamps in 1943.

CONCENTRATION CAMP GATES

Another form of gate associated with the Nazi empire were those found at concentration camps throughout the territories of the expanded Germany. A number of these bore the slogan *Arbeit macht frei* ('Work sets you free') – it appeared at Dachau, Auschwitz, Flossenbürg and Monowitz, among others. The phrase would have been in full view of the prisoners who trudged beneath it as they passed into the camps, but although it may appear to be a cruel trick and a false promise – a clumsy Nazi sleight of hand to hide the purpose of the camps – it has a serious and straightforward history.

The slogan is a corruption of a well-known quote from the Bible – '*Wahrheit macht frei*' ('The truth will set you free') – and was first coined in 1873 in the title of a novel by the German author Lorenz Diefenbach (1806–83). The protagonist of Diefenbach's novel is a wastrel and gambler who finds a path to virtue through regular employment. Diefenbach, who was closely associated with the German Nationalist movement, did not pluck this theme from obscurity, but directly from the politics around him. At the time of writing, many believed that Germany was in the grip of a moral and spiritual decline, as well as an economic one, and thought that the path to security and future glory for the empire was to be found through labour. This idea was then taken forward by both the Weimar Republic in the 1920s and the Nazis in the 1930s.

The ideology was most visibly seen in the establishment of the Reich Labour Service (*Reichsarbeitsdienst*) in 1935. Service was compulsory for all German citizens aged between eighteen and twenty-five for a minimum of six months. They provided the workforce for the huge Nazi public works programmes – including building roads, hospitals and schools, and planting forests. This worked in parallel with the Beauty of Labour (*Schönheit der Arbeit*) organization, which was launched by the Nazis in 1934 and continued until the end of the war, with the aim of improving the quality of the working experience and ensuring that more work was done for the good of the empire.

When the slogan appeared on the gates of concentration camps, therefore, it spoke directly of that very Nazi ideology – that Germany itself would find freedom through work. The first to use the phrase in the concentration camp system was Theodor Eicke, who from June 1933 to July 1934 was the commandant at Dachau, the first official concentration camp (established a matter of weeks after Hitler seized power). Eicke was also responsible for first issuing the distinctive blue-and-white striped pyjamas that came to symbolize the Nazi camps.

The gate from Auschwitz still survives at Auschwitz-Birkenau, though after the sign's theft (and subsequent recovery) in 2005 a replica now stands above the entrance of the camp itself, the original being stored in the museum. Note that the death camp next door, Birkenau, did not have the slogan on its gate – it was not necessary.

The 'Arbeit Macht Frei' sign over the entrance of the
Auschwitz concentration camp

Regardless of the intention of those Nazis who believed in the slogan and in its value at the gates of concentration camps, the prisoners had different ideas. The lettering of the phrase on the wrought-iron gate at Auschwitz is unusual: the 'B' is upside down. Historians believe that this was a deliberate act of defiance by the Polish political prisoners who made it, under the instruction of Jan Liwacz (1898–1980), a master blacksmith and a prisoner at the camp.

Kazimierz Albin, a Pole from Kraków who in 1943 was sent in the first transport to Auschwitz, as prisoner number 118, later wrote:

We were shocked by the cynicism of the Germans. They wrote 'work sets one free', although we found out for ourselves that the work at Auschwitz was only a method of killing prisoners. So we quickly put together the words '*Arbeit Macht Frei durch den Schornstein*'. This new phrase meant 'Work sets one free through the chimney'.

Auschwitz

A network of concentration and extermination camps built by Nazi Germany in occupied Poland. These included the original camp, Auschwitz I, originally built to house Polish political prisoners; Auschwitz II (Birkenau), an extermination camp equipped with large gas chambers where an estimated 1.1 million died; and Auschwitz III, a labour camp built to staff a nearby chemical and pharmaceutical company. All of the camps were built with forced labour.

Albin was one of the fortunate few to escape Auschwitz, and he returned to Kraków. His memoirs, published in 1989 as *List Gończy* ('wanted list'), offer a remarkable insight into life and forced labour in the camp. And his sentiments were shared by Aleksander Miedziejewski, a Polish prisoner from Warsaw sent to Dachau concentration camp in September 1940:

> But there was no freedom there! And from that moment it meant that hunger, hard labour, inhuman torture and death would be your inseparable companion, and freedom can only be obtained through a crematorium oven because the Dachau camp gave prisoners three months of life.

Miedziejewski survived forced labour at Dachau, where prisoners were used in the production of German armaments, and was freed in its liberation on 29 April 1945, when American troops finally walked through its gate – a major step in the final collapse of the Third Reich.

·16·
ZEN BUDDHISM

Buddhist priests giving instructions for defence air manoeuvres, c.1940

Zen Buddhism is all about Japanese military discipline...

AN EXPANDING EMPIRE

Since the last years of the nineteenth century, Japan had followed a foreign policy of aggressive expansion, fuelled by a potent form of nationalism. Victory in the First Sino-Japanese War of 1894–5 gave them control of the island of Taiwan, and a foothold in mainland China in the form of the Korean Peninsula. That territory was then extended after victory over Russia in the Russo-Japanese War of 1904–5.

Russo-Japanese War

A hugely significant moment in the rise of Japanese power, this was the first occasion in modern times that an Asian state had defeated a European one. The war was a result of Russian expansionism aimed at Manchuria and the Korean Peninsula, but the Russians were outmuscled and out-thought. The war is also notable for the Japanese surprise attack on the Russian harbour of Port Arthur, which took place on 8 February 1904 and was a direct antecedent of the attack on Pearl Harbor in 1941.

In September 1931, the Japanese invaded Manchuria and successfully detached it from the rest of China – creating a puppet state that could be ruled from Tokyo – and then pushed further north, into Mongolia. By 1942 they had also spread south and west from Manchuria and had annexed territory throughout South-East Asia, taking control of Hong Kong, Burma, Thailand, French Indochina, Malaya, the Philippines and the Dutch East Indies.

The militarism and nationalism that defined Japanese thought and behaviour in this remarkable advance was profoundly – and perhaps surprisingly – influenced by Buddhism, a religion that, perhaps more than any other, is associated with peace, compassion and serenity.

A RELIGION FOR WAR

Buddhism originated in India and travelled to China along the silk roads of Asia, before arriving in Japan at some point in the middle of the sixth century. The Buddhism that grew there shared the principal tenets and disciplines wherever it flourished: *sīla* (morality), *dhyāna* (meditation) and *prajñā* (intuitive knowledge), with an emphasis on cultural tolerance, and no conception of 'Holy War'. However, the beliefs and practices of one form of Buddhism – Zen Buddhism – also fitted very well with the requirements of the military in late-1930s Japan. *Zen* is the Japanese word for the Sanskrit *dhyāna*, usually interpreted to suggest meditation, contemplation and the concentration of the mind. It is a discipline rather than a philosophy, and it was this aspect of Buddhism that became the principal focus when Zen Buddhism developed in China.

By the 1930s, the Japanese had learned painful lessons in their wars against China and Russia. Although they had won both, it had also become clear that any future success in this new era of total war would require the mobilization of the entire country's resources, both material and human. This is where Zen fitted in, because its followers respected and practised virtues that Japanese military leaders recognized as valuable: mental discipline, self-reliance, self-denial and single-mindedness. Zen taught its disciples not to turn back once a path was decided upon; it advocated an indifference to life and death; and it taught that emotion and physical possession were encumbrances to efficiency. All of these concepts also dovetailed with the traditional Japanese warrior culture of the samurai. Zen teachings, therefore, found a ready audience in Japan when it arrived in the country in the thirteenth century. Unlike in China, it was embraced by the military class and then nurtured for seven centuries.

In the 1930s, Zen Buddhist leaders not only openly justified Japanese militarism, but also actively cooperated with the Japanese army. Zen practices were shaped into military training exercises. Regulations for life in Zen monasteries – which required keeping large numbers of men healthy, clean and orderly – directly inspired army regulations for life in camp. A report written by the infantry major Kishi Yajirō (1874–1938) in 1907, after a visit to a Zen monastery, noted that 'A basic principle should be to make it clear that all activities, whether sitting, lying down, sleeping or eating are opportunities for the soldier to cultivate his spirit.'

Zen monasteries served as a model for the army's organizational structure as well, particularly in regard to the relationship between rank and experience. In Zen monasteries, far greater importance was attached to length of training than to age, a principle also respected by the Japanese military. The integration of Zen into the Japanese military was so pervasive that, in 1944, Zen master Sawaki Kada (1880–1965) observed how Zen monasteries and military training camps 'truly resemble each other closely'. Even the Japanese army's mess kits were inspired by the monks' catering kits. This was not lost on the soldiers, who made this song popular in the ranks:

Oh how we dislike the military
With its metal teacups and metal chopsticks!
We are not Buddhas
What a pity they feed us as if we were!

Above all, however, it was the discipline of Zen that appealed to the military. The author and historian of Zen (and Zen practitioner himself) D. T. Suzuki (1870–1966) noted in his book *The Training of the Zen Buddhist Monk* (1934):

> Zen discipline is simple, direct, self-reliant, self-denying; its ascetic tendency goes well with the fighting spirit. The fighter is to be always single-minded with one object in view: to fight, looking neither backward nor sidewise. To go straight forward in order to crush the enemy is all that is necessary for him... A good fighter is generally an ascetic or stoic, which means he has an iron will. This, when needed, Zen can supply.

In the 1930s, high-ranking Zen Buddhist teachers followed government directives to fall in line with Japan's aggressive foreign policy and began to defend – if not exactly to preach – violence. In 1934, the senior Buddhist priest Gempō Yamamoto (1866–1961) declared that 'the Buddha, being absolute, has stated that when there are those who destroy social harmony and injure the polity of the state, then... killing them is not a crime'.

Zen master and teacher Daiun Sogaku Harada (1871–1961) was even more specific, writing in 1939:

> [If ordered to] march: tramp, tramp or shoot: bang, bang. This is the manifestation of the highest Wisdom [of enlightenment]. The unity of Zen and war of which I speak extends to the farthest reaches of the holy war [now under way].

The result was that, during the Second World War, violence that was inspired and sanctioned by religion became a distinct cultural characteristic of Japan – much like it had for Christian and Islamic forces during the Crusades of the Middle

Ages, another example of the harnessing of religious ideals for secular ends.

ACCEPTING RESPONSIBILITY

The full extent of Zen's complicity in Japanese military philosophy and actions was not identified by historians until the late 1990s, but it has since led to some remarkable apologies from leading figures in Japanese Zen. In September 2011, just sixteen days after Islamic extremists hijacked and flew American passenger planes into the World Trade Center and Pentagon, the leaders of one of Japan's main Zen sects, Myōshin-ji, issued a statement that was a concise acceptance of guilt, noting that 'in the past our nation, under the banner of Holy War, initiated a conflict that led to great suffering'. A subsequent and more nuanced statement specifically acknowledged how Japanese Zen leaders and institutions had lent a religious purpose to the programme of invasion and colonization that defined Japanese behaviour in the run-up to the war and then during it, leading to the destruction of '20 million precious lives'. Other institutions of Japanese Zen have since followed suit with their own admissions of culpability.

The apologetic tones of these kinds of statements are thrown into sharp focus by wartime accounts such as that of the Zen master Genjō Nakajima (1915–2000), who told his story as an eighty-four-year-old man who had risen to the ranks of abbot of Shōin-ji temple and head of the Hakuin branch of the Rinzai Zen sect. His portrayal of his wartime exploits in the Japanese navy are significant for the denial they expose. In one powerful section, he describes the capture of Nanjing in December 1937, which he witnessed first-hand as a sailor on the decks of the warship *Ise*:

> we were able to capture it without much of a fight at all. I have heard people claim that a great massacre took place at

Nanjing, but I am firmly convinced there was no such thing. It was wartime, however, so there may have been a little trouble with the women.

The events to which he refers are now known as the 'Nanjing Massacre' or the 'Rape of Nanjing', in which Japanese soldiers were responsible for the deaths of up to 300,000 civilians, and the rape of up to 20,000 women and also children. Some of these murders, in the form of mass beheadings and shootings, took place on the city's riverbanks, overlooked by Japanese navy ships, and the navy itself was responsible for murdering civilians who attempted to escape by rowing or swimming across the Yangtze River. Perhaps most striking of all was that, in the recording of his testimony, Nakajima wept and regretted the war, but he was careful to note that his tears were only for his fallen comrades:

This was a stupid war. Engulfed in a stupid war, there was nothing I could do. I wish to apologize, from the bottom of my heart, to those of my fellow soldiers who fell in battle. As I look back on it now, I realize that I was in the navy for a total of ten years. For me, those ten years felt like an eternity. And it distresses me to think of all the comrades I lost.

This passage is just one example of the silences of leaders of organized religion regarding the horrors of war. Japan is still only slowly coming to terms with the collaboration between this peace-loving religion and the unfettered violence of the Japanese war machine during the Second World War, and historians are still only starting to piece the story together.

·17·

INSECTS

Louseous Japanicas

The first serious outbreak of this lice epidemic was officially noted on December 7, 1941, at Honolulu, T. H. To the Marine Corps, especially trained in combating this type of pestilence, was assigned the gigantic task of extermination. Extensive experiments on Guadalcanal, Tarawa, and Saipan have shown that this louse inhabits coral atolls in the South Pacific, particularly pill boxes, palm trees, caves, swamps and jungles.

Flame throwers, mortars, grenades and bayonets have proven to be an effective remedy. But before a complete cure may be effected the origin of the plague, the breeding grounds around the Tokyo area, must be completely annihilated.

'Louseous Japanicas' propaganda poster published in the *Leatherneck* magazine produced by the US Marine Corps, 1945

Insects are all about mass death...

ACADEMIC WARNINGS

Awareness of the malevolent potential of insects as a cause of death and mayhem on a massive scale skyrocketed during the Second World War. And this increased awareness was encapsulated in a series of six articles written by Professor C. L. Metcalf, then head of the department of entomology at the University of Illinois, and published in a professional journal, *The Science Teacher*, in February 1943. The first began with a frankly terrifying survey of the potential for insects to cause chaos – particularly in a country whose economy and manpower were already overstretched by war. Metcalf pulled no punches. 'All who have studied [the behaviour of insects] carefully recognize that insects are mankind's greatest enemies, even in peace times', he wrote, before reminding his readers that insects were the largest and most destructive group of animals on earth.

His article outlined the potentially devastating impact of swarms of insects on resources and the ecosystem. He warned that food for humans and animals, whether growing in the fields or kept in stores, had to be protected from attack by insects – as did wool and hides, livestock and eggs. Timber, either in buildings or as essential parts of weapons such as gun stocks, also had to be protected. Above all, however, he was sanguine about the potential direct threat to humans and animals from diseases carried by insects: 'An enormous horde of these pests insists upon having the fresh warm blood of man, of our domestic animals or of fowls, as their only acceptable food.' Mosquitoes, mites, bed bugs, fleas, lice, ants and cockroaches could cause paralysing annoyance as well as fatal disease.

Metcalf used historical facts carefully to build his argument, explaining how in the Crimean War (1853–6), 1,700 British soldiers had died from wounds but more than 15,000 perished from insect-borne disease. He then explained how those numbers increased as warfare modernized and the scale of fighting forces grew. During the First World War, he wrote, louse-borne typhus was responsible for 300,000 deaths in Serbia, 2 million fatalities in Russia, and 10 million deaths in the Balkans and Ukraine in the war's aftermath.

BIOLOGICAL WEAPONS

If those figures were not shocking enough, even more so was Metcalf's assertion that now, in the midst of the Second World War, insects and enemies could be found working together. He highlighted the potential use of lice infected with typhus, mosquitoes with yellow fever, and fleas infected with bubonic plague as plausible weapons of war. He also made it clear that this would cause him no moral dilemma. 'If we must kill our enemies to restore peace to the world', he wrote:

> I do not see that it is any more sinful to kill them with
> diseases than with bombs or bullets... such warfare would
> be like scattering bombs that would not only kill at the time,
> but would live, spread and multiply a thousand-fold or more
> in succeeding years.

By 1943, the tactical use of plague-infected fleas was not just a fantasy plucked from medieval nightmare: it had already happened. Starting in 1935, in a remote area of north-western China, the Japanese had been developing biological weapons in secret and testing them on human subjects. A centre had been established for this research with the ingenuously bland name 'Unit 731'. It is now held to be the location of some of the worst war crimes ever committed. One of the weapons developed there was bubonic plague, with rats specially bred for the purpose of generating the fleas which carried the plague. The remains of Unit 731 have been preserved by the Chinese as evidence of Japanese war crimes on their soil, and can still be visited. Among the surviving buildings is a squat, dark bunker, once home to lines of cages that housed weaponized rats.

Bubonic plague

One of three forms of plague, distinctive for the raised buboes - swollen lymph nodes - that appear in the armpits and groin. It was responsible for the Black Death in the fourteenth century, in which an estimated third of the European population died. The Chinese and Japanese knew of its potency from a pandemic that began in Asia in 1855 and was possibly spread along the Silk Road, the ancient land-trade route that connected Europe and Asia. It is often transmitted by the bite of an infected rat flea, a parasite of rodents.

In October 1940, a plague-weapon was first tried in anger when Japanese planes flew over two Chinese cities: Ningbo, a port near Shanghai, and Quzhou, an inland transhipment centre positioned at the confluence of two major rivers from which maritime trade carried goods deep into inland China. The attack did not bring juddering explosions but a gentle rain of organic material – rice, wheat and chaff – and clinging to those stalks and husks were fleas infected with bubonic plague.

The Chinese were by no means ignorant of the likelihood of such an attack, however. Although the response in Quzhou was chaotic, in Ningbo it was impressive – it was focused, coordinated and effective. A quarantine area where the infected material had landed was designated, and a brick wall was built around it with a curved section of sheet metal atop the wall to stop the area's rats – which might now host the plague-infected fleas – from escaping. A moat was then built around the wall and the entire area was disinfected with steamed sulphur and then razed to the ground, ultimately cleansed by fire. The infected and potentially infected were monitored; 23,343 people were vaccinated; financial rewards were paid for catching or killing rats; and newspapers even published advice that included rat-catching tips. The entire city was brought together as a community in the face of this insect threat. Nonetheless, the terrifying potential of this weapon was proved: the death rate of those infected in the attacks ranged from 92 to 98 per cent.

EXTERMINATION

The plague-bombing of these cities did not escape the intelligence network of the Americans, and it added to a growing portfolio of horrifying facts about Japanese behaviour – which was seen as brutal, perverse and excessive. In response to these insect-borne attacks, the American intelligence community, politicians and troops came to embrace the metaphor of the Japanese themselves as insects, deserving nothing less than extermination. The American wartime reporter Ernie Pyle, who had begun the war embedded with troops in Europe, was profoundly shocked by his later experiences of war in the Pacific – and in particular with his new enemy. In February 1945, he wrote:

> In Europe we felt our enemies, horrible and deadly as they were, were still people. But out here I soon gathered that the Japanese were looked upon as something subhuman and repulsive; the way some people feel about cockroaches or mice.

In the same piece he went on to describe how, shortly after arriving, he saw a group of Japanese prisoners in a wire-fenced courtyard. He noted how they were 'wrestling and laughing and talking just like normal human beings. And yet they gave me the creeps and I wanted a mental bath after looking at them.'

Ernie Pyle (1900–45)

A Pulitzer Prize-winning American journalist and war correspondent who focused not on the movement of armies or the decisions of generals but on the experience of the common soldier. His articles appeared in newspapers across the country, with a readership of millions. Being mentioned in a Pyle article became a measure of outstanding achievement, akin to receiving a medal. He covered campaigns in North Africa and Italy, as well as the Normandy invasions and the Pacific war. Pyle was killed by enemy fire at the Battle of Okinawa in the spring of 1945. His death was mourned publicly by Eleanor Roosevelt in her regular newspaper column, 'My Day' (see p. 120).

Numerous similar descriptions – and evidence of a desire to 'exterminate' the Japanese – survive from this period in US military accounts; in various sources the Japanese were viewed as spiders, scorpions, lice and ants. A particularly telling cartoon from *Leatherneck,* a magazine for the US Marines, shows a hideous, hairy, horned, toothy insect with Asiatic eyes, the rising sun at the end of its whip-like tail, and the star found on the Japanese army's hats and helmets in the centre of its forehead. The beast is named 'Louseous Japanicas', and the text that accompanies it notes that it has 'breeding grounds around the

Tokyo area' and that it 'must be completely annihilated'. The 'first serious outbreak', the text claims, 'was officially noted on December 7, 1941, at Honolulu' (referring to the Japanese attack on Pearl Harbor). Since then, 'To the Marine corps, especially trained in combating this type of pestilence, was assigned the gigantic task of extermination.' It continues in more detail:

> Extensive experiments on Guadalcanal, Tarawa, and Saipan have shown that this louse inhabits coral atolls in the South Pacific, particularly pill boxes, palm trees, caves, swamps and jungles. Flame throwers, mortars, grenades and bayonets have proven to be an effective remedy.

Such rhetoric is reminiscent of the more widely known Nazi propaganda about Jews, which also repeatedly cast them as insects: spiders, swarms of locusts, leeches and worms. Blurring the lines between insects, vermin and disease, Hitler himself called Jews 'carriers of bacilli worse than Black Death', and Josef Goebbels declared:

> Since the flea is not a pleasant animal we are not obliged to keep it, protect it and let it prosper so that it may prick and torture us, but our duty is rather to exterminate it. Likewise with the Jew.

The way that the lines blurred between propaganda and practice in both of these cases is well known. In Japan it led to the mass fire-bombing of major cities and the subsequent atomic bombing of Hiroshima and Nagasaki, resulting in the deaths of up to a quarter of a million Japanese civilians; and in Germany to the 'extermination' of 6 million Jews. It is no coincidence that the first experiments at Auschwitz on the techniques of mass human gassing utilized crystals of an insecticide called Zyklon B – which had been left behind at the camp by an insect extermination company. It was found to be so effective that it was mass-produced for use in death camps. One prosecutor at the Nuremberg trials testified that enough Zyklon B had been sent to Auschwitz alone to kill 'millions of human beings'.

·18·
DEAFNESS

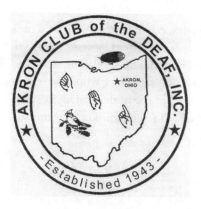

Badge of the Akron Club of the Deaf, Inc., established 1943

Deafness is all about lost stories...

Historians have only recently begun to uncover the experiences of deaf people during the Second World War, and they are discovering countless lost stories that profoundly enrich our understanding of the war – in both its light and its shade.

STERILIZATION AND MURDER

The deaf were persecuted by the Nazis as a means to purify the German race. Nazi doctors examined those with hearing difficulties and determined who should be sterilized or forbidden to marry, who could live 'free', who would be sent to a concentration camp and who should die in dedicated 'hospital' killing centres as part of the *Aktion T4* euthanasia programme.

Aktion T4

A post-war name for a Nazi medical programme in which doctors selected patients deemed to be 'incurably sick' for euthanasia. The main criterion was economic: could the patient contribute to the German economy? The programme began in September 1939 and continued until the end of the war, resulting in the deaths of up to 300,000 disabled, mentally ill, elderly and infirm, as well as many deaf people. The extermination centres were located in psychiatric hospitals, and were antecedents of the gas chambers subsequently built in concentration camps.

Some questioned the rights of deaf German children to an education, considering it a waste of resources. Historical research has now revealed that, between 1933 and 1945, 17,000 deaf Germans were sterilized and around 2,000 deaf children were killed by lethal injection or starvation. Women suspected of carrying a deaf foetus were forced to undergo abortions.

This attitude towards people with disabilities was by no means shared by all in Germany, however, and some came to the assistance of their fellow citizens. Otto Weidt (1883–1947), the owner of a brush-making and broom-binding workshop in Berlin, secured status for his workshop as essential to the war effort, and employed as many as thirty blind and deaf Jews. He then went to extraordinary lengths to protect his workforce – falsifying documents, hiding them and even bribing Gestapo officers hunting for Jews and the disabled.

SILENT COLONIES

In America, by contrast, the war opened doors for some deaf Americans that might have otherwise been shut. Good hearing was a medical requirement for soldiers joining up, and was also a requirement for women to join the WAACS and WAVES. The armed forces developed a series of complicated tests to identify those who faked deafness as a means of avoiding conscription – what the authorities described as 'malingering in hearing'. But for those men and women who were genuinely deaf, employment opportunities now arose on the home front.

The rubber factories of Akron, Ohio, were a notable employer of the deaf, so much so that Akron became known as the 'Cross-roads of the Deaf' and the nation's largest 'silent colony'. This, however, had not suddenly begun with the Second World War. The foundations had already been laid by both the Firestone and Goodyear corporations, who had recruited significant numbers of deaf workers to Akron during the First World War. This in turn had built on an initiative in the first decade of the twentieth century, when the Ohio State Labor Bureau encouraged factories to employ deaf workers. During the First World War, over 150 deaf workers were employed there in the tyre-finishing department, overseen by a hearing supervisor skilled at sign language.

WAACS and WAVES

The Women's Army Auxiliary Corps (WAACS) and the Women Accepted for Volunteer Emergency Service (WAVES) were the women's branches of the US army and navy respectively. More than 150,000 women served in the WAACS during the war, and around 86,000 joined the WAVES.

By the time demand for rubber increased again during the Second World War, therefore, there was already a significant history of deaf employment in Akron, and in the subsequent years around 800 deaf men and women were employed by Goodyear and Firestone. At Firestone the recruitment was encouraged by Benjamin Schowe Sr, a labour economics research specialist with the company who was himself deaf and who had fought for deaf people's employment rights against insurance companies and government agencies during the Great Depression.

Deaf men and women came to the city from as far afield as California, Florida, South Dakota, Montana and Texas. Their jobs were varied and – like their hearing counterparts – were usually semi-skilled, though some were placed in skilled or professional positions and supervisory roles, including overseeing the development of and relations between the 'silent community' and the rest of the workforce. The companies who employed them organized a variety of social, business and phil-anthropic activities for both their hearing and deaf workers. They also provided the deaf with club rooms, dance halls and sports facilities, allowing them the opportunity to socialize with others who shared their own language and life experi-ences. The deaf community themselves also worked together. Deaf women, in particular, formed clubs and led numerous group and charity efforts such as a drive to raise money for sick and elderly deaf adults.

But Akron was now no longer unique in offering employ-ment opportunities to deaf citizens, and one statistic stands out: during the war, the number of firms interested in hiring deaf employees exceeded the number of deaf adults looking for work. An example of other recruiters of the deaf was the Milwaukee Ordnance Plant in Milwaukee, Wisconsin, which manufactured .50 calibre machine-gun cartridges, and from 1942 operated twenty-four hours a day, six days a week. The man put in charge of overseeing the operation was Colonel Arthur M. Wolff.

Before the war, Wolff had been a board member of the Institu-tion for the Improved Instruction of Deaf Mutes in New York City, and in his role at the plant he used the opportunity to employ deaf women to work in a team at the end of the production line, as inspectors of the ordnance. Interviewed in a local newspaper, Wolff argued for their value, saying: 'Noise does not distract them. There is never any idle conversation, and they generally have the steel will to succeed on the job with steady and hard work.' The factory's production was immense, and these women played an integral part in guaranteeing the quality of the ammu-nition produced. The *Milwaukee Journal* reported gleefully on 29 September 1943 how: 'Enough cartridges have been made at the plant to kill everyone in the United States.'

The experience of deaf workers like these was heralded by proponents of disabled workers in the years after the Second World War. 'Each deaf workman [at Akron]', wrote Benjamin Schowe Sr in 1959, 'is like a man with lantern on a moonless night. He dispels the gloom or prejudice all around him, and others can see the gleam of his light from afar.'

The war thus created energy and optimism among the deaf community, and a hope that the war might have sparked a lasting change; that it might have led to some long-term good. They had worked towards the future from the outset, knowing that the war would not last forever.

In practice, however, that expectation was not met, and they continued to labour against formidable systemic obstacles in the workplace – as well as in society at large. The author of a contemporary US government handbook *Aid to the Physically Handicapped* (1945) summed up their wartime change of fortune with the biting line: 'The deaf come into their rights only when the world is in a midst of a terrible human holocaust.'

ATOMIC BOMBS

Historians are now intent on recovering the testimonies of deaf people during the Second World War, and one of the most moving archives being created is made up of deaf accounts of the atomic bombings of Hiroshima and Nagasaki.

Meiko Higashi was born in Nagasaki unable to hear. Her account of 9 August 1945 was recorded – with the help of the Nagasaki branch of the Japanese Study Group of Sign Language Problems – when she came for a physical screening test for atomic bomb survivors held annually in the city. During breaks in the medical tests, she began to communicate using simple gestures and basic sign language. Her skill at signing was limited, and she had neither received an education nor worked with interpreters before. She was unable to write anything other than her name or read anything but the simplest of words – 'pen' or 'hat' – which made it very challenging to express herself in a way that was understood by others. This was the first time her story had ever been told, and it came out piece by piece in ten interpretation sessions.

The atomic bombings of Hiroshima and Nagasaki

On 6 August 1945, a uranium-235 atom bomb was dropped by a US plane on the Japanese city of Hiroshima, the first time that a nuclear weapon had been used in war. Three days later, another nuclear weapon, though of a different type (plutonium), was dropped on Nagasaki. An estimated 80,000 people immediately died in Hiroshima and 40,000 in Nagasaki, though neither incident was as destructive as the more traditional bombing raid carried out on Tokyo in March of that year, which killed some 100,000.

Over the course of this time, she revealed that she was in Motohara at the time of the bombing, only a mile from the hypo-centre – making her one of very few survivors at such close range. The nine-year-old Meiko had been in her house, looking after her younger sister and playing marbles on the floor, when the bomb exploded. She saw a white flash and then was blown to the ground by a hot wind and pinned under heavy tatami mats. The house was full of debris, and now leaned to one side. Her sister was alive but trapped under matting. Meiko recalled looking at the sky, saying:

> There was an orange-coloured ball of fire surrounded by whirlpools of moving white smoke. The clouds soon became long and narrow and spread out like wings. Flashes of red light snorted out through cracks in the clouds. I was so frightened that my body shook uncontrollably.

Her two other siblings now ran inside, horribly burned, and then her mother appeared, the skin on her chest 'dripping down like melted wax'. They ran to an air-raid shelter in the nearby mountainside. The following days were dominated by headaches, diarrhoea, an overpowering stench, and maggots appearing in her mother's burns. Several days later the family walked seven miles into the mountains to stay with relatives. Meiko's mother died. Her youngest brother died. Her sister died. She was split up from her other two siblings. She settled in the mountains but was forced to work the fields, harvesting potatoes. She was ridiculed and beaten by the local children because she was deaf. When she told this part of the story, she hit herself as hard as she could in the face, repeatedly – so traumatized was she by her experiences.

Meiko subsequently took the interpreters who had helped her tell her story on a tour of Nagasaki and led them to the house of an elderly lady, Mrs Ide, one of only a handful of living people whom Meiko had known in her childhood before the bomb. Meiko's spoken vocabulary was almost non-existent, but when she laid eyes on Mrs Ide she called out in a clear voice 'Oba-chan', which means 'Grandma'. They then prayed together in front of the family's Buddhist altar, and wept.

·19·
SUICIDE

A Japanese kamikaze plane flies into the USS *Missouri* during
the Battle of Okinawa, 1945

Suicide is all about loyalty...

Suicide rates went down during the Second World War, though accounts of suicide are prevalent in so many accounts that it comes across as a prominent feature of the conflict. It was a means to escape the horrors of warfare, the pain of bereavement, the misery of occupation, defeat or imprisonment – but we also see in the war numerous examples of suicide as the ultimate act of loyalty, a form of self-sacrifice that was bound up with honour and a sense of duty.

KAMIKAZE

During the final stages of the war in the Pacific, over 3,800 pilots of the Japanese Imperial army and navy had died as kamikaze in hostile operations, causing the deaths of some 7,000 Allied naval personnel. The term *kamikaze* translates as 'divine wind', and during this period these Japanese Special Attack Units of military aviators flew single-seat airplanes loaded with explosives into enemy warships, in a manner that was far more effective than conventional aerial or underwater attacks. The Japanese also employed other suicide craft, including boats, submarines, and even divers who stuck mines to the bottom of enemy ships.

Kamikaze aircraft were used to good effect against the Allied Pacific fleet, with the intention of demonstrating the determination of the Japanese war effort and deterring the Allies from embarking on a land invasion. One of the first phases of these attacks was during the Battle of Okinawa in April–June 1945, when Japanese airmen flew a wave of special missions targeting Allied destroyers and aircraft carriers and inflicted damage on the fleet. Although no carriers were actually sunk during this conflict, many were badly damaged and suffered high numbers of casualties, including HMS *Formidable*, HMS *Victorious* and HMS *Howe*, and the American carriers USS *Franklin* and USS *Bunker Hill*. *Bunker Hill* was struck by two kamikaze pilots, setting the ship on fire and causing over 600 casualties and 346 fatalities, with 43 more missing in action. Despite the damage inflicted, she was intact enough to struggle home to the US mainland.

Japanese Special Attack Units

Special Attack Units (known as *tokkōtai* or *shimbu-tai*) were formed by the Imperial navy and army to undertake suicide missions towards the end of the war in the Pacific, when Japan were anticipating US attacks on the mainland. The deployment of troops willing to sacrifice their own lives had proved extremely effective in the Philippines in 1944, and this suicide tactic was used for the rest of the war. The benefit was that Japan could use a relatively small but exceedingly committed force to destroy enemy targets.

Something of the impact of these tactics on US sailors is captured in the Pacific war diaries of James Fahey, a seaman first class aboard the cruiser USS *Montpelier*, a vessel that came under aerial attack on 27 November 1944 while it was part of an eighteen-strong task force. Fahey explained how the ships moved into defensive formation, circling round a fuel tanker while they took it in turns to refuel. During this time they were bombarded from the skies by suicide planes, which showered them with machine-gun fire, dropped their payloads and dive-bombed them:

Jap planes were coming at us from all directions. Before the attack started we did not know that they were suicide planes, with no intention of returning to their base. They had one thing in mind and that was to crash into our ships, bombs and all... The Jap planes were falling all around us, the air was full of Jap machine gun bullets. Jap planes and bombs were hitting all around us. Some of our ships were being hit by suicide planes, bombs and machine gun fire. It was a fight to the finish.

Something of the context for the kamikaze culture can be found in the pamphlet *Kokutai No Hongi* (*Fundamentals of our National Polity*) produced by the Ministry of Education in 1937. A group of academics had been commissioned to write on the 'national essence' of Japan; to create an official ideology for a country on the brink of war. In it, the rationale for taking one's own life for the good of Japan was clearly expressed:

Hence, offering our lives for the sake of the Emperor does not mean so-called self-sacrifice but the casting aside of our little selves to live under his august grace and the enhancing of the genuine life of the people of a state...

This was not mere government rhetoric. First-hand testimony of Japanese pilots planning to fly their planes into enemy ships survives in numerous diary accounts, wills and correspondence with family members. Such personal documents reveal insights into why these young men were prepared to die for the good of their country.

Representative of these extraordinarily personal documents is a letter dated 1 June 1945, from Corporal Takao Adachi to his grandmother and his father, written immediately prior to taking off from Giran airfield in Taiwan. Only seventeen years of age, he was a member of the 20th *Hikō Sentai* ('Flying Regiment'), and on his death he was promoted to second lieutenant. In his letter home, Adachi thanks his family for their great kindness in raising him, saying that he had 'not been able to do anything to repay' their kindness, but that:

Living as a man in this divine country that faces an extreme emergency, in my heart I am absolutely satisfied that I have a good place to die as a member of the Special Attack Corps Makoto Hikōtai.

He further added 'I am determined that I certainly will carry out a certain-death, certain-kill [*hisshi hissatsu*] body-crashing [*taiatari*] attack and instantly sink an enemy ship.'

This and similar suicide notes express a profound loyalty to Imperial Japan, and the sense of honour with which these men acted. Analysing the accounts collectively, the authors rationalize their own deaths as defending the country and its people, in response to devastating Allied air raids on the Japanese homeland. And taking their own lives was an act of filial piety to their own parents. It also demonstrated their strong sense of solidarity with other pilots, as well as their firm sense of honour and responsibility, and hatred of cowardice.

MASS NAZI SUICIDE

The sacrificial suicides of these Japanese servicemen can be contrasted with the mass suicides that took place in Nazi Germany in the last months of the war, when thousands of German citizens, officials and military personnel took their own lives out of a mixture of fear, loyalty to the regime and loyalty to their partners or comrades. The suicides began in early January 1945 as Soviet troops advanced, forcing the Germans back towards their homeland. This was followed by another phase of suicides in April and May. As the Red Army reached the East German town of Demmin, more than 1,000

Germans killed themselves and sometimes their children; and in 1945, at least 7,000 Berliners, many of them ordinary citizens, were reported dead at their own hands. These months also saw several top-ranking Nazi party officials taking their own lives – including Hitler and his propaganda minister Josef Goebbels, whose wives also committed suicide, with Magda Goebbels killing her children with cyanide tablets.

The Death of Adolf Hitler

The leader of the German Nazi party killed himself in his underground bunker by gunshot on 30 April 1945, followed shortly afterwards by his wife Eva Braun, who died having taken a cyanide capsule. In accordance with his final instructions, both their bodies were carried into the Reich Chancellery garden, doused in petrol and set alight to prevent them falling into enemy hands.

Many had killed themselves because they feared the inevitable reprisals that would come in the aftermath of a German defeat – fears fed by Nazi propaganda, which warned of rape, torture and death at the hands of the advancing Red Army. A Nazi leaflet dating from February 1945 warned Germans of a 'Bolshevik murderer-pack' that, in the event of an Allied victory, would unleash 'incredible hatred, looting, hunger, shots in the back of the neck, deportation and extermination'.

Yet for others, suicide was in keeping with a long-established indoctrination that fostered loyalty to the Nazi regime. Many felt that it was preferable to die in defeat than suffer the ignominy of occupation by a foreign power, and this was very much in line with Nazi propaganda – which since early in the war had espoused this view. In a speech to the Reichstag in 1939, at the time of the invasion of Poland, Hitler expressed his preference for suicide over capitulation:

> I now wish to be nothing other than the first soldier of the German Reich. Therefore I have put on that tunic which has always been the most holy and dear to me. I shall not take it off again until after victory is ours, or I shall not live to see the day!

In a military briefing in August 1944 he was even clearer, arguing publicly in favour of suicide: 'It's only [a fraction] of a second. Then one is redeemed of everything and finds tranquillity and eternal peace.'

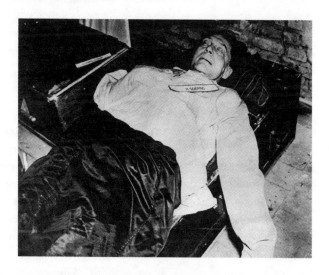

The body of Hermann Goering who committed suicide
on 5 November 1946

·20·
RUBBLE

Women in Berlin, East Germany, clearing up rubble after the
devastation of World War II, 1945

Rubble is all about post-war rehabilitation...

RUBBLE WOMEN

The war transformed the appearance of those European cities that had been bombed or become the front line of street-to-street fighting. Roads were blocked by piles of rubble; wonky towers of bricks that had once been buildings stood like broken teeth against the skyline. In Germany this posed a twofold problem. On the one hand the apocalyptic landscapes needed to be cleared to make way for a new Germany; on the other, the sapling strength of the German male workforce of the 1930s had been broken by the war – there were now simply too few men available to undertake the work. During the war a similar problem had presented itself, and some rubble had been cleared by prisoners of war or minority groups interned by the Germans, as well as soldiers and the Hitler Youth.

The solution was to recruit women to do the work – to use female power to lay a path for a new world – and the Allied powers in Germany ordered all women between the ages of fifteen and fifty to help with the post-war clean-up. These women acquired a name – *Trümmerfrauen* ('rubble women') – and they took to the streets, moving rubble by hand, digging up mounds, breaking up blocks with hammers and taking debris away in carts. As many as 60,000 women were mobilized in Berlin alone, and an unknown number (but likely to be in the millions) across all of Germany. Historians estimate that they cleared 500 million cubic metres of rubble from around Germany's cities.

Their work was celebrated at the time by propagandists working for the new Germany, who used images of groups of smiling working women to recruit others to the task. But these are carefully constructed images. One notable example shows a chain of women handing debris down an angled line from the apex of a mountain of rubble just out of picture. They smile and laugh, joy bubbling over at their task. Some wear floral dresses, to achieve the most powerful contrast between the winter of the world in the background and the spring of the people in the foreground; they are a new shoot of life in the city's wasteland.

Personal accounts from the women themselves, however, cast a darker light on their experiences. When she was ninety-two, Helga Cent-Velden recorded her experiences working as an eighteen-year-old rubble woman in Berlin, clearing a ruin:

> The house had been hit by a bomb and the whole inside had collapsed. And I was there to clear it all up with just one other woman, who had worked there when the building was still standing... So we started to clear all the rubble away. We had no tools. I brought some metal buckets from home, the kind that were normally used to transport foodstuffs like sauerkraut or gherkins or jam. So we put the bits of rubble into those buckets and carried them out to a tipping trolley... For the really large bits like beams and very heavy pieces of debris we had some help but otherwise it was just the other woman and me who dismantled that huge pile. I wore some kind of gloves to avoid injury because all that rubble was jagged and dangerous. I was lucky – I got away without any major injuries.

The idea of these hard-working and apparently happy-go-lucky rubble women has been used repeatedly by German politicians in the subsequent years. In a speech in Munich in 2005, former German chancellor Helmut Kohl called the *Trümmerfrauen* 'a symbol of the German people's wish to rebuild and of their powers of survival'. They even still exist in some German cities in physical form. A statue in Dresden, raised in 1952, for example, shows one such woman, striding forward, hammer in hand – a moment of fortitude, hope and strength, forever cast in bronze.

RUBBLE FILMS

Another way that the rubble in German cities was used by propagandists was in film; and, like the rubble women, this phenomenon was also given a special name: *Trümmerfilme* or 'rubble films'.

The film industry in post-war Germany itself rose from the rubble of war, and it had unique characteristics as its rehabilitation was overseen by the occupying Allied forces. There were certain requirements imposed on German filmmakers. Films were not to include any sense of militarism or national pride, but they were to address directly the gravity of the nation's mistakes – not just during the war but for the entire twelve years of Nazi rule.

The films are strikingly similar to each other in their use of rubble landscapes as a powerful metaphor for ruined lives and psychological trauma. *The Murderers Are Among Us* (1946) was the first *Trümmerfilm*, and was granted a licence by the Soviets after the authorities in the British, French and American occupation zones refused to approve it. The film is set in Berlin, where more than half of the city's flats and houses had been destroyed and more than a million made homeless. It opens in a shattered landscape dotted with makeshift graves, children playing in the dirt, people wandering in shadows – all set to the unsettling jingle of a bar-room piano. The disorientation is jarring but then becomes profound. A woman arrives at the railway station, and makes her way through the rubble to the building where she used to live. She finds an old acquaintance, an optician in the shop on the ground floor. Things appear to be normal in this world of the abnormal, but then she climbs her stairs and finds a strange man living in her flat, who has simply claimed an abandoned set of rooms as his own.

Scene from *The Murderers Are Among Us* (1946)

Before they meet at her front door, the man is shown rummaging through her wardrobe and drawers. When they speak at her threshold he is aggressive and sinister, though he allows her in. The scene ends with her putting her suitcase in a shattered room. Looking over her shoulder she says plaintively, 'I hope we get along.' Dismissive, the man does not reply. This confrontation between the two at the very opening of the film puts centre stage a moral and legal conflict concerning the ownership of dispossessed property, property theft and vagrancy that was faced by thousands of Germans after the war.

With troubling personal themes like this – along with powerful broader questions about crime on a national scale – the film was immensely successful. It was released just two weeks after twenty-four major war criminals were tried at the Nuremberg trials, twelve of whom were sentenced to death. The executions were carried out the day after the premiere. Over 6 million people saw the film and it was screened in twenty-three countries. *The Murderers Are Among Us* was a narrative of its age set among the rubble of the previous, part of an important step in Europe's rehabilitation.

The Nuremberg trials

A series of trials held in 1945-6 in which former Nazi leaders were tried as war criminals by the International Military Tribunal. Among a number of significant precedents set, the court rejected the contention that only a state – and not individuals – could be found guilty of war crimes. Twelve were sentenced to death by hanging, seven received prison sentences, three were acquitted and two not charged.

A TRANSATLANTIC BROTHERHOOD

In Britain and America, rubble created an opportunity to celebrate their Allied brotherhood in a unique way, and later aided in the forging of post-war bonds. American ships and shipping were common sites in many British port cities during the war, but particularly so in Bristol, where American convoys carrying equipment for the Normandy invasions docked. Bristol was one of the British cities that was heavily targeted by the Luftwaffe in the air war, and was faced with the monumental task of clearing its rubble.

The solution was clever. American aid ships came in, heavily loaded with goods. The ships were unloaded in Bristol but this made them unsafe for their transatlantic return journey, as their stability was compromised. The solution was to load the rubble from Bristol's bombed houses, churches, pubs, shops and warehouses into the holds of the American ships to act as ballast. Some 3,000 miles later – now safely across the Atlantic – the rubble was unloaded in Manhattan and put to good use, serving as the foundations for an area of the borough reclaimed from the East River near East 52nd Street.

To make certain that Bristol's contribution to the building of New York – as well as America's contribution to the winning of the war – was not forgotten, the area was named 'Bristol Basin', and a plaque was set up that reads, in part:

These fragments that once were homes shall testify while men love freedom to the resolution and fortitude of the people of Britain. They saw their homes struck down without warning... It was not their walls but their valor that kept them free...

Below this inscription is a verse from the poem *America* by Bayard Taylor (1825–78), an American poet who travelled widely and spent significant time in England:

And broad-based under all
Is planted England's oaken-hearted mood
As rich in fortitude
As e'er went worldward from the island wall.

JOIN IN!

We believe passionately that everyone – not just professional historians – can effectively exercise their historical imagination. If you have a great idea for a *Histories of the Unexpected* subject, fill in one of these forms, photograph it and send it to us

on Twitter @UnexpectedPod

or by email to **info@historiesoftheunexpected.com** and we might dedicate a podcast episode to you and your historical imagination!

The history of _____ is all about...

_____

The history of _____ is all about...

_____

The history of _____ is all about...

_____

The history of _____ is all about...

_____

The history of _____ is all about...

_____

SELECTED FURTHER READING

___

GENERAL READING

Beevor, Antony, *The Second World War* (London: Weidenfeld & Nicolson, 2012).

Cantwell, John D., *The Second World War: A Guide to Documents in the Public Record Office* (3rd edition) (London: PRO Publications, 1993).

Churchill, Sir Winston, *The Second World War* (abridged edition) (London: Cassell, 1958).

Dear, I. C. B., and M. R. D. Foot, eds, *The Oxford Companion to World War II* (Oxford: Oxford University Press, 1995).

Devine, Louis Paul, 'The British Way of War in North West Europe 1944–45: A Study of Two Infantry Divisions' (unpublished PhD thesis, University of Plymouth, 2013).

Evans, Richard, *The Third Reich in Power 1933–1939* (New York: Penguin Press, 2005).

Gilbert, Martin, *The Second World War: A Complete History* (New York: Henry Holt and Company, 1989).

Jones, Dan, and Marina Amaral, *The Colour of Time: A New History of the World, 1850–1960* (London: Apollo, 2018).

Noakes, Lucy, and Juliette Pattinson, eds, *British Cultural Memory and the Second World War* (London: Bloomsbury, 2014).

Overy, Richard, ed., *The Oxford Illustrated History of World War II* (Oxford: Oxford University Press, 2015).

——————, *Why the Allies Won* (New York: W. W. Norton & Company, 1997).

Parker, R. A. C., *Second World War: A Short History* (Oxford: Oxford Paperbacks, 2002).

Taylor, A. J. P., *The Origins of the Second World War* (London: Hamish Hamilton, 1961).

Taylor, Peter, *Weird War Two: Intriguing Items and Surprising Stuff from the Second World War* (London: Imperial War Museums, 2017).

The Wartime Memories Project, https://www.wartimememories. co.uk/ [accessed 15.11.2018].

Weinberg, Gerhard L., *World War II: A Very Short Introduction* (Oxford: Oxford University Press, 2014).

———, *A World at Arms: A Global History of World War II* (2nd edition) (Cambridge: Cambridge University Press, 2005).

1. BLOOD

Buscemi, Francesco, 'Edible Lies: How Nazi Propaganda Represented Meat to Demonise the Jews', *War, Media and Conflict*, 9/2 (August 2016), pp. 180–97.

Guglielmo, Thomas A., '"Red Cross, Double Cross": Race and America's World War II-Era Blood Donor Service', *The Journal of American History*, 97/1 (June 2010), pp. 63–90.

Mills, Mary, 'Propaganda and Children During the Hitler Years', https://www.yadvashem.org/download/education/conf/Millsishedwithoutpic.pdf [accessed 30.11.18].

'Parliamentary Speeches', Hansard, House of Commons 5th series, 5th October 1938 c.360–371, https://api.parliament.uk/historic-hansard/commons/1938/oct/05/policy-of-his-majestys-government#column_360 [accessed 30.11.18].

———, 13 May 1940 'His Majesty's Government', https://api.parliament.uk/historic-hansard/commons/1940/may/13/his-majestys-government-1 [accessed 30.11.18].

Sax, B., *Animals in the Third Reich: Pets, Scapegoats and the Holocaust* (New York: Continuum, 2000).

Toye, Richard, *The Roar of the Lion: The Untold Story of Churchill's World War II Speeches* (Oxford: Oxford University Press, 2013).

2. KING ARTHUR

Dunsany, Lord, *War Poems* (London: Hutchinson, 1941).

Harty, Kevin J., 'King Arthur Goes to War (Singing, Dancing, and Cracking Jokes): Marcel Varnel's 1942 Film *King Arthur Was a Gentleman*', *Arthuriana*, 14/4 (Winter 2004), pp. 17–25.

Lacy, Norris J., 'King Arthur Goes to War', in Debra N. Mancoff, ed., *King Arthur's Modern Return* (New York: Garland, 1998), pp. 159–69.

Richmond, Velma Bourgeois, 'King Arthur and His Knights for Edwardian Children', *Arthuriana*, 23/3 (Fall 2013), pp. 55–78.

Simpson, Roger, 'King Arthur in World War Two Poetry: His Finest Hour?', *Arthuriana*, 13/1 (Spring 2003), pp. 66–91.

Traxler, Janina P., 'Once and Future Saxons: Nazis and Other Dark Forces in the Modern Arthurian Story', *Arthuriana*, 11/4 (Winter 2001), pp. 96–107.

Wheeler, Bonnie, 'The Masculinity of King Arthur: From Gildas to the Nuclear Age', *Quondam et Futurus*, 2/4 (Winter 1992), pp. 1–26.

3. CANCER

Caplan, Arthur L., ed., *When Medicine Went Mad: Bioethics and the Holocaust* (Totowa, NJ: Humana Press, 1992).

Cocks, Geoffrey, 'Sick Heil: Self and Illness in Nazi Germany', *Osiris*, 22/1 (2007), pp. 93–115.

Davey Smith, George, 'Lifestyle, Health, and Health Promotion in Nazi Germany', *British Medical Journal*, 329/7480 (2004), p. 1424.

———, S. A. Ströbele and M. Egger, 'Cigarette Smoking and Health Promotion in Nazi Germany', *Journal of Epidemiology and Community Health*, 51/2 (April 1997), pp. 208–10.

Morabia, Alfredo, 'Anti-Tobacco Propaganda: Soviet Union Versus Nazi Germany', *American Journal of Public Health*, 107/11 (November 2017), pp. 1708–10.

Proctor, Robert N., *The Nazi War on Cancer* (Princeton, NJ: Princeton University Press, 2000).

———, 'The Nazi War on Tobacco: Ideology, Evidence, and Possible Cancer Consequences', *Bulletin of the History of Medicine*, 71/3 (February 1997), pp. 435–88.

———, 'The Anti-Tobacco Campaign of the Nazis: A Little Known Aspect of Public Health in Germany, 1933–45', *British Medical Journal*, 313/7070 (December 1996), pp. 1450–3.

Schneider, Nick K., and Stanton A. Glantz, '"Nicotine Nazis Strike Again": A Brief Analysis of the Use of Nazi Rhetoric in Attacking Tobacco Control Advocacy', *Tobacco Control*, 17/5 (October 2008), pp. 291–6.

4. CARROTS

Beckett, Ian F. W., *The Home Front 1914–1918: How Britain Survived the Great War* (Kew: The National Archives, 2006).

Ginn, Franklin, 'Dig For Victory! New Histories of Wartime Gardening in Britain', *Journal of Historical Geography*, 38/3 (2012), pp. 294–305.

Hammond, R. J., *Food and Agriculture in Britain, 1939–45: Aspects of Wartime Control* (Stanford, CA: Stanford University Press, 1954).

Harvey, D., and M. Riley, '"Fighting from the Fields": Developing the British "National Farm" in the Second World War', *Journal of Historical Geography*, 35/3 (July 2009), pp. 495–516.

Middleton, C. H., *Digging for Victory: Wartime Gardening with Mr Middleton* (London: Aurum Press, 2008).

'Parliamentary Debate on Rationed Foodstuffs', Hansard, House of Commons Debate, 30 September 1941, Vol. 374, cc. 473–5, https://api.parliament.uk/historic-hansard/written-answers/1941/sep/30/rationed-foodstuffs [accessed 05.12.18].

Rose, S., *Which People's War? National Identity and Citizenship in Wartime Britain, 1939–1945* (Oxford: Oxford University Press, 2003).

Sitwell, William, *Eggs or Anarchy: The Remarkable Story of the Man Tasked with the Impossible: To Feed a Nation at War* (London: Simon & Schuster, 2016).

Smith, Daniel, *The Spade as Mighty as the Sword: The Story of World War Two's Dig for Victory Campaign* (London: Aurum Press, 2011).

Smith, K. Annabelle, 'A WWII Propaganda Campaign Popularized the Myth That Carrots Help You See in the Dark', *Smithsonian Magazine*, https://www.smithsonianmag.com/arts-culture/a-wwii-propaganda-campaign-popularized-the-myth-that-carrots-help-you-see-in-the-dark-28812484/ [accessed 05.12.18].

Stolarczyk, John, 'Carrots in the Second World War', World Carrot Museum, http://www.carrotmuseum.co.uk/history4.html [accessed 04.12.18].

Wiggam, Marc Patrick, 'The Blackout in Britain and Germany during the Second World War' (unpublished D.Phil thesis, University of Exeter, 2011).

---

5. MOZART

Aber, Adolf, 'Music and Politics in the Third Reich', *Musical Times*, 85 (1944), pp. 179–80.

Bergmeier, Horst P. J., and Rainer E. Lotz, eds, *Hitler's Airwaves: The Inside Story of Nazi Radio Broadcasting and Propaganda Swing* (New Haven, CT: Yale University Press, 1997).

Etlin, Richard A., ed., *Art, Culture, and Media Under the Third Reich* (Chicago: University of Chicago Press, 2002).

Kater, Michael, 'Forbidden Fruit? Jazz in the Third Reich', *The American Historical Association*, 94/1 (February 1989), pp. 11–43.

Levi, Eric, *Mozart and the Nazis: How the Third Reich Abused a Cultural Icon* (New Haven, CT: Yale University Press, 2010).

Morris, John V., 'Battle for Music: Music and British Wartime Propaganda 1935–1945' (unpublished PhD thesis, University of Exeter, 2011).

Potter, Pamela M., 'What Is "Nazi Music"?', *The Musical Quarterly*, 88/3 (Autumn 2005), pp. 428–55.

———, 'Musicology under Hitler: New Sources in Context', *Journal of the American Musicological Society*, 49/1 (Spring 1996), pp. 70–113.

6. DARKNESS

Bell, Amy, 'Landscapes of Fear: Wartime London, 1939–1945', *Journal of British Studies*, 48/1 (January 2009), pp. 153–75.

Calder, Angus, *The People's War: Britain 1939–45* (London: Panther, 1971).

Field, Geoffrey, 'Nights Underground in Darkest London: The Blitz, 1940–1941', *International Labor and Working-Class History*, 62 (Fall 2002), pp. 11–49.

Gardiner, Juliet, *The Blitz: The British Under Attack* (London: Harper Press, 2010).

Mannheim, Hermann, *Group Problems in Crime and Punishment* (London: Routledge, 1955).

———, 'Crime in Wartime England', *The Annals of the American Academy of Political and Social Science*, 217/1 (September 1941), pp. 128–37.

Parliament UK, 'Look Out in the Blackout', https://www.parliament.uk/business/publications/research/olympic-britain/transport/look-out-in-the-blackout/ [accessed 27.02.19].

Slater, Stefan Anthony, 'Containment: Managing Street Prostitution in London, 1918–1959', *Journal of British Studies*, 49/2 (2010), pp. 332–57.

Smith, Harold L., *Britain in the Second World War: A Social History* (Manchester: Manchester University Press, 1996).

Sudlow, Roy, *I Remember it Well: Memoirs of an Ordinary Man* (Lulu.com, 2008).

Szreter, Simon, and Kate Fisher, *Sex before the Sexual Revolution: Intimate Life in England, 1918–1963* (Cambridge: Cambridge University Press, 2010).

Wiggam, Marc Patrick, 'The Blackout in Britain and Germany During the Second World War' (unpublished MA thesis, University of Exeter, 2011).

7. CARS

Flink, James J., 'Three Stages of American Automobile Consciousness', *American Quarterly*, 24/4 (1972), pp. 451–73.

Frohardt-Lane, Sarah, 'Promoting a Culture of Driving: Rationing, Car Sharing, and Propaganda in World War II', *Journal of American Studies*, 46/2 (May 2012), pp. 337–55.

Hastings, Max, *The Secret War: Spies, Codes and Guerrillas 1939–1945* (London: William Collins, 2015).

Leong, Adam, *Killing the Enemy: Assassination Operations During World War II* (London: I.B. Tauris, 2015).

Pyta, Wolfram, Nils Havemann and Jutta Braun, *Porsche: From an Engineering Office to a Global Brand* (Munich: Siedler, 2017).

Rieger, Bernhard, *The People's Car: A Global History of the Volkswagen Beetle* (Cambridge, MA: Harvard University Press, 2013).

Taylor, Blaine, *Volkswagen Military Vehicles of the Third Reich* (Cambridge, MA: Da Capo Press, 2004).

8. POCKETS

Boris, Eileen, 'Desirable Dress: Rosies, Sky Girls, and the Politics of Appearance', *International Labor and Working Class History*, 69/1 (Spring 2006), pp. 123–42.

Burman, Barbara, and Seth Denbo, 'The History of Pockets', https://www.vads.ac.uk/texts/pockets/history_of_tie-on_pockets.pdf [accessed 19.11.18].

Davis, Brian L., *Uniforms and Insignia of the British Army* (Arms & Armour, 1983).

Delano, Page Dougherty, 'Making Up for War: Sexuality and Citizenship in Wartime Culture', *Feminist Studies*, 26/1 (February 2000), pp. 33–68.

Gordon, David, *Uniforms of the WWII Tommy* (Pictorial Histories Publishing Company, 2005).

Hall, Martha L., Belinda T. Orzada and Dilia Lopez-Gydosh, 'American Women's Wartime Dress: Sociocultural Ambiguity Regarding

Women's Roles During World War II', *The Journal of American Culture*, 38/3 (September 2015), pp. 232–42.

Jewell, Brian, *British Battledress 1937–61* (Oxford: Osprey Press, 1992).

Lubitz, Rachel, 'The Weird, Complicated, Sexist History of Pockets', https://mic.com/articles/133948/the-weird-complicated-sexist-history-of-pockets#.lVfVDtzSq [accessed 19.11.18].

McKay, Brett and Kate, 'A Man's Pockets', *The Art of Manliness Blog*, https://www.artofmanliness.com/articles/a-mans-pockets/ [accessed 19.11.18].

Snodgrass, Mary Ellen, *World Clothing and Fashion: An Encyclopedia of History, Culture, and Social Influence* (London: Routledge, 2014).

Twinch, Carol, *Women on the Land: Their Story During Two World Wars* (Cambridge: Lutterworth Press, 1990).

Unsworth, Rebecca, 'Hands Deep in History: Pockets in Men and Women's Dress in Western Europe, c. 1480–1630', *Costume*, 51/2 (2017), pp. 148–70.

Victoria and Albert Museum, 'A History of Pockets', V&A Blog, http://www.vam.ac.uk/content/articles/a/history-of-pockets/ [accessed 19.11.18].

9. FURNITURE

'Air Raids in London', https://www.bbc.co.uk/history/ww2peopleswar/stories/89/a2756289.shtml [accessed 18.01.19].

Attfield, J., '"Give 'em Something Dark and Heavy": The Role of Design in the Material Culture of Popular British Furniture, 1939–1965', *Journal of Design History*, 9/3 (1996), pp. 185–201.

Brown, Mike, and Carol Harris, *The Wartime House* (Stroud: The History Press, 2011).

Edwards, C. D., *Twentieth-century Furniture: Materials, Manufacture and Markets* (Manchester: Manchester University Press, 1994).

Erenberg, Lewis A., and Susan E. Hirsch, eds, *The War in American Culture: Society and Consciousness During World War II* (Chicago: University of Chicago Press, 1996).

Frank, Anne, *The Diary of a Young Girl: The Definitive Edition*, ed. Otto H. Frank and Mirjam Pressler, trans. Susan Massotty (London: Doubleday, 1991).

Grayzel, Susan, *At Home and Under Fire: Air Raids and Culture in Britain from the Great War to the Blitz* (Cambridge: Cambridge University Press, 2012).

Mills, J., *The 1943 Utility Furniture Catalogue with an Explanation of Britain's Second World War Utility Furniture Scheme* (Sevenoaks: Sabrestorm Publishing, 2008).

Morrison, Herbert, *An Autobiography* (London: Odhams Press, 1960).

Reimer, Suzanne, and Philip Pinch, 'Geographies of the British government's wartime Utility furniture scheme, 1940–1945', *Journal of Historical Geography*, 39 (2013), pp. 99–112.

United States Holocaust Museum, 'Personal Stories: Hiding', https://www.ushmm.org/exhibition/personal-history/media_oi.php?MediaId=1230&th=hiding [accessed 20.11.18].

Wade, Stephen, *Air-Raid Shelters of World War II: Family Stories of Survival in the Blitz* (Barnsley: Remember When, 2011).

Werman, Marco, 'This Jewish Couple Survived the Holocaust Hidden Behind a Church Organ', PRI The World, 27 November 2015, https://www.pri.org/stories/2015-11-27/jewish-couple-survived-holocaust-hidden-behind-church-organ-their-daughter-also [accessed 20.11.18].

World Holocaust Remembrance Center, 'In Cellars, Pits and Attics', https://www.yadvashem.org/yv/en/exhibitions/righteous/hiding.asp [accessed 20.11.18].

---

10. MOTHERS

Angolia, John R., *For Führer and Fatherland: Political & Civil Awards of the Third Reich* (San Jose, CA: R. James Bender Pub., 1989).

Brashler, Karin Lynn, 'Mothers for Germany: A Look at the Ideal Woman in Nazi Propaganda' (unpublished MA dissertation, Iowa State University, 2015).

Hall, Allan, 'Revealed: Begging Letters for Nazi "Mother Cross"', *The Scotsman*, 13 May 2014, https://www.scotsman.com/news/world/revealed-begging-letters-for-nazi-mother-cross-1-3408486 [accessed 27.11.18].

Jeansonne, Glen, *Women of the Far Right: The Mothers' Movement and World War II* (Chicago: University of Chicago Press, 1997).

McEnaney, Laura, 'He-Men and Christian Mothers: The America First Movement and the Gendered Meanings of Patriotism and Isolationism', *Diplomatic History*, 18/1 (1994), pp. 47–57.

Mouton, Michelle, *From Nurturing the Nation to Purifying the Volk – Weimar and Nazi Family Policy, 1918–1945* (Cambridge: Cambridge University Press, 2007).

Thane, Pat, and Tanya Evans, 'The Second World War: Another Moral Panic', in *Sinners? Scroungers? Saints?: Unmarried Motherhood in Twentieth-Century England* (Oxford: Oxford University Press, 2012), pp. 54–81.

11. PUPPETS

Alvarez, Alexander, 'Adjusting to Genocide: The Techniques of Neutralization and the Holocaust', *Social Science History*, 21/2 (Summer 1997), pp. 139–78.

Ancel, Jean, 'The German-Romanian Relationship and the Final Solution', *Holocaust and Genocide Studies*, 19/2 (Fall 2005), pp. 252–75.

Astles, Cariad, 'Swazzles of Subversion: Puppets Under Dictatorship', in Patrick Duggan and Lisa Peschel, eds, *Performing (for) Survival: Theatre, Crisis* (London: Palgrave Macmillan, 2016), pp. 103–20.

Balfour, M., ed., *Theatre and War 1933–1945: Performance in Extremis* (Oxford: Berghahn Books, 2001).

Blumenthal, E., *Puppetry and Puppets* (London: Thames & Hudson, 2005).

Brustein, William I., and Ryan D. King, 'Balkan Anti-Semitism: The Cases of Bulgaria and Romania Before the Holocaust', *East European Politics and Societies*, 18/3 (2004), pp. 430–54.

Deletant, Dennis, *Hitler's Forgotten Ally: Ion Antonescu and his Regime, Romania 1940–44* (New York: Palgrave Macmillan, 2006).

Jurkowski, H., *A History of European Puppetry: Volume Two: The Twentieth Century* (Lewiston, NY: Edwin Mellen Press, 1996).

Myrsiades, Linda Suny, 'Greek Resistance Theatre in World War II', *The Drama Review*, 21/1 (1977), pp. 99–106.

United States Holocaust Memorial Museum, https://www.ushmm.org/ [accessed 27.03.19].

12. COWS

Bentley, A., *Eating for Victory: Food Rationing and the Politics of Domesticity* (Urbana, IL: University of Illinois Press, 1998).

Boissoneault, Lorraine, 'When the Nazis Tried to Bring Animals Back From Extinction', https://www.smithsonianmag.com/history/when-nazis-tried-bring-animals-back-extinction-180962739/ [accessed 29.11.18].

Buscemi, Francesco, 'Edible Lies: How Nazi Propaganda Represented Meat to Demonise the Jews', *War, Media and Conflict*, 9/2 (2016), pp. 180–7.

Bushill, A., '"Nazi" Cattle being Bred in UK', BBC News, 26 April 2009, http://news.bbc.co.uk/2/hi/uk_news/8019029.stm [accessed 29.11.18].

Davidson, A., *The Oxford Companion to Food* (2nd edition) (Oxford: Oxford University Press, 2006).

Driessen, Clemens, and Jamie Lorimer, 'Back-Breeding the Aurochs: The Heck Brothers, National Socialism and Imagined Geographies for Nonhuman Lebensraum', in P. Giaccaria and C. Minca, eds, *Hitler's Geographies* (Chicago: University of Chicago Press, 2016), pp. 138–57.

Food Facts for the Kitchen Front (London: Harper Press, 2009).

Ganzel, Bill, 'The Livestock Industry Grows During the 1940s', Wessels Living History Farm, York, Nebraska, https://livinghistoryfarm.org/farminginthe40s/crops_08.html [accessed 29.11.18].

Harrington, Lisa M. B., and Max Lu Harrington, 'Beef Feedlots in Southwestern Kansas: Local Change, Perceptions, and the Global Change Context', *Global Environmental Change*, 12 (2002), pp. 273–82.

Heck, Lutz, *Animals: My Adventure* (London: Methuen, 1954).

Lorimer, Jamie, and Clemens Driessen, 'From "Nazi Cows" to Cosmopolitan "Ecological Engineers": Specifying Rewilding Through a History of Heck Cattle', *Annals of the American Association of Geographers*, 106 (2016), pp. 631–52.

Mac Con Iomaire, Máirtín, and Pádraic Óg Gallagher, 'Irish Corned Beef: A Culinary History', *Journal of Culinary Science & Technology*, 9/1 (2011), pp. 27–43.

Mintz, S. W., *Tasting Food, Tasting Freedom: Excursions into Eating, Culture, and the Past* (Boston, MA: Beacon Press, 1996).

Murray, Williamson, and Allan Reed Millett, *A War to Be Won: Fighting the Second World War* (Cambridge, MA: Belknap Press, 2009).

Orland, B., 'Turbo-cows: Producing a Competitive Animal in the Nineteenth and Early Twentieth Centuries', in S. Schrepfer and P. Scranton, eds, *Industrializing Organisms* (London and New York: Routledge, 2004), pp. 167–90.

Paisaje Industrial Fray Bentos, Official Fray Bentos Heritage Site (Spanish language website), http://paisajefraybentos.com/pc/ [accessed 27.03.19].

Saito, I., and N. Yagasaki, 'Development of Cattle Feedlots and Vertical Integration of Beef Industry in the American High Plains', *Journal of Geography*, 107/5 (1998), pp. 674–94.

Sax, B., *Animals in the Third Reich: Pets, Scapegoats and the Holocaust* (London: Continuum, 2000).
UNESCO, 'Fray Bentos Industrial Landscape', https://whc.unesco.org/en/list/1464 [accessed 27.03.19].

13. HANDKERCHIEFS

Baldwin, R. E., 'Silk Escape Maps: Where Are They Now?', *Mercator's World* (Jan–Feb 1998), pp. 50–1.
Beavan, Colin, *Operation Jedburgh: D-Day and America's First Shadow War* (New York: Viking, 2006).
Bond, Barbara A., *Great Escapes: The Story of MI9's Second World War Escape and Evasion Maps* (London: Times Books, 2015).
———, 'MI9's Escape and Evasion Mapping Programme, 1939–1945' (unpublished PhD thesis, University of Plymouth, 2014).
——————, 'Escape and Evasion Maps in WWII and the Role Played by MI9', *The Ranger*, 2/19 (Summer 2009).
———, 'Silk Maps: The Story of MI9's Excursion into the World of Cartography, 1939-1945', *The Cartographic Journal*, 21/2 (1984), pp. 141–3.
———, 'Maps Printed on Silk', *The Map Collector*, 22 (1983), pp. 10-13.
Doll, John G., *Cloth Maps of World War II: Western Association of Map Libraries*, WAML, *Information Bulletin*, 20/1 (November 1988).
Hall, Debbie, 'Wall Tiles and Free Parking: Escape and Evasion Maps of World War II', *British Library* (April 1999), http://www.mapforum.com/04/escape.htm [accessed 27.03.19].
Neave, Airey, *They Have Their Exits* (London: Hodder & Stoughton, 1953).
Nichol, John, and Tony Rennell, *The Last Escape: The Untold Story of Allied Prisoners of War in Germany 1944–45* (London: Viking, 2002).
Nichols, Major Ralph D., *Jedburgh Operations: Support to the French Resistance in Eastern Brittany* (undated).
'Stories from the Men of Phantom-Operation Houndsworth', https://www.bbc.co.uk/history/ww2peopleswar/stories/18/a6115718.shtml [accessed 18.03.19].

14. PAPERBACKS

Ballou, R. O., *A History of the Council on Books in Wartime, 1942–1946* (New York: Country Life Press, 1946).

Cole, John Young, *Books in Action: The Armed Services Editions* (Washington, DC: Library of Congress, 1984).

Davis, Kenneth C., *Two-Bit Culture: The Paperbacking of America* (Boston, MA: Houghton Mifflin, 1984).

Hench, John B., *Books as Weapons: Propaganda, Publishing, and the Battle for Global Markets in the Era of World War II* (Ithaca, NY: Cornell University Press, 2010).

Manning, Molly Guptill, *When Books Went to War* (Boston, MA: Houghton Mifflin Harcourt, 2014).

Merveldt, Nikola von, 'Books Cannot Be Killed by Fire: The German Freedom Library and the American Library of Nazi-Banned Books as Agents of Cultural Memory', *Library Trends*, 55/3 (Winter 2007), pp. 523–35.

Poole, Alex H., '"As Popular as Pin-Up Girls": The Armed Services Editions, Masculinity, and Middlebrow Print Culture in the Mid-Twentieth-Century United States', *Information & Culture*, 52/4 (2017), pp. 462–86.

Schick, Frank Leopold, *The Paperbound Book in America; The History of Paperbacks and their European Background* (New York: R. R. Bowker Co., 1958).

Travis, Trysh, 'Books as Weapons and "The Smart Man's Peace": The Work of the Council on Books in Wartime', *The Princeton University Library Chronicle*, 60/3 (1999), pp. 353–99.

15. GATES

CYARK, 'Brandenburg Gate: A National Icon', https://www.cyark.org/projects/brandenburg-gate [accessed 07.12.18].

Delbo, Charlotte, *Auschwitz and After*, trans. Rosette C. Lamont (New Haven, CT: Yale University Press, 1995).

Discover Cracow, 'Arbeit Macht Frei', https://discovercracow.com/arbeit-macht-frei/ [accessed 21.01.19].

Friedman, Régine-Mihal, 'The Double Legacy of Arbeit Macht Frei', *Prooftexts*, 22/1–2 (2002), pp. 200–20.

Hagen, J., 'Architecture, Symbolism, and Function: The Nazi Party's

"Forum of the Movement"', *Environment and Planning D: Society and Space*, 28/3 (2010), pp. 397–424.

Heyck, Hartmut, 'Labour Services in the Weimar Republic and Their Ideological Godparents', *Journal of Contemporary History*, 38/2 (2003), pp. 221–36.

'Kazimierz Albin', Auschwitz-Birchenau Memorial and Museum, http://auschwitz.org/en/museum/auschwitz-council/iac-members/kazimierz-albin/ [accessed 21.01.19].

Langer, Lawrence, *Holocaust Testimonies: The Ruins of Memory* (New Haven, CT: Yale University Press, 1991).

LeValley Kama'ila, Linda, 'Poetry and History: Reflections of Stanley Diamond's "Arbeit Macht Frei"', *Dialectical Anthropology*, 24 (1999), pp. 293–304.

Reeve, William C., 'Kleist's Hermannsschlacht and the Brandenburger Tor', *Seminar: A Journal of Germanic Studies*, 27/2 (1991), pp. 95–101.

Roth, John K., 'Holocaust Business: Some Reflections on Arbeit Macht Frei', *The Annals of the American Academy of Political and Social Science*, 450/1 (1980), pp. 68–82.

Schneider, Bernhard, 'Invented History: Pariser Platz and the Brandenburg Gate', *AA Files*, 37 (Autumn 1998), pp. 12–16.

16. ZEN BUDDHISM

Abe, M., *Zen and Comparative Studies* (Basingstoke: Palgrave, 1997).

Fumihiko, Sueki, 'Chinese Buddhism and the Anti-Japan War', *Japanese Journal of Religious Studies,* 37/1, Religion and the Japanese Empire (2010), pp. 9–20.

Heft, James L., ed., *Beyond Violence: Religious Sources of Social Transformation in Judaism, Christianity, and Islam* (New York: Fordham University Press, 2004).

Ives, Christopher, *Imperial-Way Zen: Ichikawa Hakugen's Critique and Lingering Questions for Buddhist Ethics* (Honolulu: University of Hawai'i Press, 2009).

Suzuki, Daisetz Teitaro, *The Training of the Zen Buddhist Monk* (Kyoto: Eastern Buddhist Society, 1934).

Victoria, Brian Daizen, *Zen War Stories* (London: Routledge, 2012).
———, *Zen at War* (New York: Rowman & Littlefield, 2006).

17. INSECTS

Cushing, Emory C., *History of Entomology in World War II* (Washington, DC: Smithsonian Institution, 1957).

Harris, Sheldon H., *Factories of Death: Japanese Biological Warfare, 1932–1945, and the American Cover-Up* (London: Routledge, 2002).

Guillemin, Jeanne, *Hidden Atrocities: Japanese Germ Warfare and American Obstruction of Justice at the Tokyo Trial* (New York: Columbia University Press, 2017).

Jeans, Roger B., Jr, 'Alarm in Washington: A Wartime "Exposé" of Japan's Biological Warfare Program', *The Journal of Military History*, 71/2 (2007), pp. 411–39.

Metcalf, C. L., 'Importance of Insects in War Time', *The Science Teacher*, 11/1 (1944), pp. 20–2, 40, 42.

Perkins, John H., 'Reshaping Technology in Wartime: The Effect of Military Goals on Entomological Research and Insect-Control Practices', *Technology and Culture*, 19/2 (April 1978), pp. 169–86.

Russell, Edmund P., '"Speaking of Annihilation": Mobilizing for War against Human and Insect Enemies, 1914–1945', *The Journal of American History*, 82/4 (1996), pp. 1505–29.

Schoppa, R. Keith, *In a Sea of Bitterness: Refugees during the Sino-Japanese War* (Cambridge, MA: Harvard University Press, 2011).

Tanaka, Toshiyuki, *Hidden Horrors: Japanese War Crimes in World War II* (Lanham, MD: Rowman & Littlefield, 2017).

18. DEAFNESS

Anon, *Aid to the Physically Handicapped* (US Government Printing Office, 1945).

Buchanan, Robert M., *Illusions of Equality: Deaf Americans in School and Factory, 1850–1950* (Washington, DC: Gallaudet University Press, 1999).

——, 'Building a Silent Colony: Life and Work in the Deaf Community of Akron, Ohio from 1910 through 1950', in Carol J. Erting et al., eds, *The Deaf Way: Perspectives from the International Conference on Deaf Culture* (Washington, DC: Gallaudet University Press, 1994), pp. 250–60.

Foster, William B. et al., *Physical Standards in World War II* (Medical Department, United States Army, 1967).

Moran, Rachel Louise, *Governing Bodies: American Politics and the Shaping of the Modern Physique* (Philadelphia, PA: University of Pennsylvania Press, 2018).

National Association of the Deaf, USA, https://www.nad.org/ [accessed 27.03.19].

Poore, Carol, *Disability in Twentieth-Century German Culture*, (Ann Arbor, MI: University of Michigan Press, 2007).

Rochester Institute of Technology, 'Deaf People and WWII', https://www.rit.edu/ntid/ccs/deafww2/ [accessed 27.03.19].

Ryan, Donna F., and John S. Schuchman, eds, *Deaf People in Hitler's Europe* (United States Holocaust Memorial Museum, 2002).

Stone, Emma, 'Life Unworthy of Life: Experiences of Deaf People in Nazi Germany', *Deaf History Journal*, 7/3 (2004), pp. 41–2.

Swanson, Carl, 'Deaf Workers Aided War Effort', *Milwaukee Notebook*, https://milwaukeenotebook.com/2015/08/18/deaf-workers/ [accessed 27.03.19].

Takeshi, Mamezuka, *Don ga Kikoenakatta Hitobito: The Deaf and the Atomic Bomb* (Kyoto, Japan: Bunrikaku, 1991).

Wheeler, David C., 'Physical Standards in Allied and Enemy Armies During World War II', *Military Medicine*, 130/9/1 (1965), pp. 899–916.

---

19. SUICIDE

Beisel, David R., 'The German Suicide, 1945', *Journal of Psychohistory*, 34/4 (2007), pp. 302–13.

Bourke-White, Margaret, 'Suicides: Nazis Go Down to Defeat in a Wave of *Selbstmord*', *Life Magazine*, 14 May 1945.

Chiran Tokkō Irei Kenshō Kai (Chiran Special Attack Memorial Society), *Konpaku no kiroku: Kyū rikugun tokubetsu kōgekitai chiran kichi* (Record of Departed Spirits: Former Army Special Attack Corps Chiran Base) (Chiran Town, Kagoshima Prefecture: Chiran Tokkō Irei Kenshō Kai, 2004; revised edition 2005).

Dower, John, *War Without Mercy: Race and Power in the Pacific War* (New York: Random House, 1987).

Earhart, Davie, 'All Ready to Die: Kamikazefication and Japan's Wartime Ideology', *Critical Asian Studies*, 37/4 (2005), pp. 569–96.

Fahey, James, *Pacific War Diary 1942–1945* (Boston, MA: Houghton Mifflin, 1963).

Goeschel, Christian, 'Suicide in Nazi Concentration Camps, 1933–9', *Journal of Contemporary History*, 45/3 (2010), pp. 628–48.

————, *Suicide in Nazi Germany* (Oxford: Oxford University Press, 2009).

Huber, Florian, *Promise Me You'll Shoot Yourself: The Mass Suicide of Ordinary Germans in 1945* (Melbourne, Australia: Text Publishing, 2019).

Inuzuka, Ako, 'Memories of the Tokko: An Analysis of the Chiran Peace Museum for Kamikaze Pilots', *Howard Journal of Communication*, 27/2 (2016), pp. 1–22.

Kamikaze Images, 'Letters, Poems, Diaries and Other Writings', http://www.kamikazeimages.net/writings/adachi/index.htm [accessed 07.12.18].

Lester, D., 'Suicide Rates: Before, during and after the World Wars', *European Psychiatry*, 9 (1994), pp. 262–4.

————, and Bijou Yang, 'The Influence of War on Suicide Rates', *The Journal of Social Psychology* (1992), pp. 135–7.

Le Tissier, Tony, *Berlin Then and Now* (London: Battle of Britain Prints, 1997).

Ohnuki-Tierney, Emiko, *Kamikaze, Cherry Blossoms, and Nationalism: The Militarization of Aesthetics in Japanese History* (Chicago: University of Chicago Press, 2002).

'Selections from the *Kokutai no hongi* (*Fundamentals of Our National Polity*), 1937', in Wm. Theodore de Bary, Carol Gluck and Arthur E. Tiedemann, eds, *Sources of Japanese Tradition,* 2nd ed., vol. 2 (New York: Columbia University Press, 2005), pp. 968–9, 975.

Tanaka, Yuki, 'Japan's Kamikaze Pilots and Contemporary Suicide Bombers: War and Terror', *The Asia Pacific Journal*, 3/7 (2005), pp. 1–6.

20. RUBBLE

Apel, Linde, 'Voices from the Rubble Society: "Operation Gomorrah" and Its Aftermath', *Journal of Social History*, 44/4 (July 2011), pp. 1019–32.

BBC, 'Berlin's Rubble Women', https://www.bbc.co.uk/programmes/w3cswsjp [accessed.27.03.19].

Carter, Erica, 'Sweeping up the Past: Gender and History in the Postwar German Rubble Film', in Ulrike Sieglohr, ed., *Heroines Without Heroes: Reconstructing Female National Identities in European Cinema, 1945–1951* (London: Cassell, 2000) pp. 91–110.

Heineman, Elizabeth, 'The Hour of the Woman: Memories of

Germany's "Crisis Years" and West German National Identity', *The American Historical Review*, 101/2 (April 1996), pp. 354–95.

Moeller, Robert G., 'The "Remasculinization" of Germany in the 1950s: Introduction', *Signs*, 24/1 (1998), pp. 101–6.

Paeslack, Miriam, 'High-Speed Ruins: Rubble Photography in Berlin, 1871–1914', *Future Anterior*, 10/2 (2013), pp. 33–47.

Rentschler, Eric, 'The Place of Rubble in the Trümmerfilm', *New German Critique*, 37/2/110 (2010), pp. 9–30.

Scholz, Natalie, 'Reordering the Material of the Past: Gender and the Morality of Things in Early Postwar Germany', *Clio: Women, Gender, History*, 2/40 (2014), pp. 80–104.

Shandley, Robert R., *Rubble Films: German Cinema in the Shadow of the Third Reich* (Philadelphia, PA: Temple University Press, 2001).

Treber, Leonie, *Mythos Trümmerfrauen: von der Trümmerbeseitigung in der Kriegs- und Nachkriegszeit und der Entstehung eines deutschen Erinnerungsortes* (Essen: Klartext Verlag, 2014).

Wickham, Christopher, 'Postwar Tales of Two Cities: Rubble Films from Berlin and Munich', *Film Criticism*, 38/3 (March 2014), pp. 24–47.

ILLUSTRATION CREDITS

p. 1 'We Can Do It!', 1943 (*Pictorial Press Ltd/Alamy Stock Photo*); p. 9 Anti-Semitic article in *Der Stürmer*, Number 14, 1937 (*Public domain*); p. 17 Scene from *King Arthur Was a Gentleman*, 1942 (*Everett Collection Inc/Alamy Stock Photo*); p. 27 Nazi anti-smoking propaganda poster (*Public domain*); p. 35 'Doctor Carrot' poster (*Public domain*); p. 41 German stamp commemorating 150th anniversary of the death of Wolfgang Amadeus Mozart (*Max Right/Alamy Stock Photo*); p. 49 'BLACKOUT means BLACK' poster, c.1942 (*Library of Congress*); p. 57 Hitler with Dr Porsche at the launch of the VW Volkswagen Beetle, May 1938 (*Shawshots/Alamy Stock Photo*); p. 60 US poster about gasoline and rubber rationing, 1942 (*Northwestern University Library*); p. 65 Woman wearing a Land Army uniform (*Herbert Gehr/The LIFE Images Collection via Getty Images*); p. 73 Anne Frank's house (*Photo 12/Alamy Stock Photo*); p. 77 A Morrison shelter (*Wikimedia Commons*); p. 81 The Cross of Honour of the German Mother (*Stephen French/Alamy Stock Photo*); p. 91 Puppet of a Jewish man in prison uniform (*United States Holocaust Memorial Museum Collection, Gift of the Katz Family*); p. 99 Illustration of an aurochs from Sigismund von Herberstein's *Rerum Moscoviticarum Comentarii*, 1556 (*Wikimedia Commons*); p. 107 Silk escape map (*Wikimedia Commons*); p. 115 Armed Services Edition of *The Great Gatsby* (*Library of Congress*); p. 123 German war-time stamp (*Shawshots/Alamy Stock Photo*); p. 125 Hitler at the parade for his fiftieth birthday celebrations (*ullstein bild via Getty Images*); p. 129 Entrance to Auschwitz concentration camp (*akturer/Shutterstock*); p. 133 Buddhist priests giving instructions for defence air manoeuvres, c.1940 (*Alinari via Getty Images*); p. 141 'Louseous Japanicas' propaganda poster, 1945 (*Public domain*); p. 149 Badge of the Akron Club of the Deaf, Inc. (*Public domain*); p. 157 Japanese kamikaze plane attacks USS *Missouri*, May 1945 (*ullstein bild via Getty Images*); p. 163 Body of Hermann Goering, 1946 (*Photo 12/Alamy Stock Photo*); German women clearing up debris and rubble, 1945 (*Popperfoto via Getty Images*); p. 169 Scene from *The Murderers Are Among Us*, 1946 (© *Progress Film-Verleih*)

While every effort has been made to contact copyright-holders of illustrations, the authors and publisher would be grateful for information about any illustrations where they have been unable to trace them, and would be glad to make amendments in further editions.

INDEX